From the Margins to the Mainstream

Enhancing Social Awareness in the Social Studies Classroom

Edited by Kenneth Cushner
Joanne Kilgour Dowdy

ROWMAN & LITTLEFIELD EDUCATION
A division of
ROWMAN & LITTLEFIELD
Lanham • Boulder • New York • Toronto • Plymouth, UK

Published by Rowman & Littlefield Education
A division of Rowman & Littlefield
4501 Forbes Boulevard, Suite 200, Lanham, Maryland 20706
www.rowman.com

10 Thornbury Road, Plymouth PL6 7PP, United Kingdom

British Library Cataloguing in Publication Information Available

Library of Congress Cataloging-in-Publication Data

Cushner, Kenneth.
From the margins to the mainstream : enhancing social awareness in the social studies classroom /
Kenneth Cushner and Joanne Kilgour Dowdy.
p. cm.
Includes bibliographical references.
ISBN 978-1-4758-0892-6 (cloth : alk. paper) -- ISBN 978-1-4758-0893-3 (pbk. : alk. paper) -- ISBN
978-1-4758-0894-0 (electronic)
1. Social sciences--Study and teaching--United States--Activity programs. 2. Group identity--Study
and teaching--United States--Activity programs. 3. Multicultural education--Activity programs. I.
Dowdy, Joanne Kilgour. II. Title.
LB1584.C78 2014
372.83--dc23

2013049336

∞™ The paper used in this publication meets the minimum requirements of American
National Standard for Information Sciences Permanence of Paper for Printed Library
Materials, ANSI/NISO Z39.48-1992.

Printed in the United States of America

Contents

Introduction

Kenneth Cushner and Joanne Kilgour Dowdy

Life is a stage and we are the actors
And everybody have a part to play
Like a never-ending movie
With all different characters
Each one have a role to portray
Down to the scavengers and them barristers
All them doctors and lawyers and these ministers
So this honourable this and this honourable that
And this Lady So and So
Is a part all these people playing
Ah want you to know

—Brother Valentino, "Calypsonian," 1972

The social studies as well as the broader area referred to as the cultural or social foundations of education have approached teaching toward social change through democratic participation and collective action since the days of John Dewey. Central to this idea is exposing students to a curriculum that encourages them to become critical inquirers who are capable and willing to investigate, reflect, and then act in a manner that builds a society that better serves the interests and needs of all people—especially those who have been traditionally marginalized due to their race, socioeconomic status, gender, sexual orientation, or their physical or mental ability.

To be intentional about creating an environment where students of any background and socioeconomic description can find a way to identify with each other and also to appreciate the differences that they represent is the way of teachers who are committed to social justice. It is a path that believes, without reservation, that each person is a microcosm of the society at large, that each has her or his place, and that the contributions of all are essential if we are to truly achieve the democratic ideals that lie at the foundation of our democratic nation. Social-justice approaches in education have become a focus through which a number of teacher education programs attempt to address these issues with teachers and ultimately children.

It is broadly recognized that much needs to change in terms of teacher education if we are to help our students more effectively address the redistribution of power and forms of control across multiple sectors of society. There is little evidence, however, to support the notion that a social justice approach to teacher education as it is currently implemented has had the desired impact (Schoorman & Bogotch, 2010; Pittman, 2009). Some critiques report that such efforts are, in large part, rhetorical in nature, with educators succumbing to political pressures where the primary emphasis has become the preparation of teachers to substantially improve K–12 academic achievement as validated through standardized testing (McDonald & Zeichner, 2009).

Many of the obstacles in the path to achieving social justice in teacher education can be traced to the relative lack of intercultural exposure, experience, understanding, and sensitivity of most teacher education students (Cushner, 2011). While it is understood that simply facilitating intercultural understanding and dialogue in and of itself does not lead directly to social reconstruction, facilitating the intercultural awareness, sensitivity, and competence of teachers can often serve as the precursor that is necessary before such change can occur.

Addressing these issues in a less confrontational and accusatory manner works to open one's mind to understanding that other perspectives, experiences, and histories can and do exist. We also know that significant experience followed by reflection is essential for any meaningful intercultural understanding and learning to occur. A multipronged and substantially more hands-on approach than that which is typically found in teacher education programs is required if we are to see the changes so badly needed and sought by so many.

This book brings together a collection of twenty-three hands-on activities designed to engage the individual in real-life and/or simulated classroom experiences that raise awareness and provide a foundation to stimulate introspection, reflection, and discussion around often sensitive issues. Faculty in schools of education as well as teachers who teach a variety of age levels and content areas have submitted activities and lessons they have found to be successful at allowing the individual to slowly acquire a level of comfort in discussing relevant and often challenging issues, consider their implications, and then to propose action-oriented strategies for change.

This book is divided into two general sections, although it also supports the companion volume by Dowdy and Cushner. Section 1 presents twelve activities that address social justice through the social studies and sciences. Activities here focus on the ways in which society constructs policies and accepted "norms" that may enhance the power of some people while diminishing the efficacy of others. Cushner's activity opens the section by asking students to become futurists—looking into both what their own future will be as well as where they envision the world to be heading, challenging them to recognize the interconnectedness they share with others around the world.

Among the activities that follow, three of the authors, Lash, Miller Marsh, and Kroeger, focus attention on the early childhood years, both in terms of socialization within the family and how early childhood teachers can be more inclusive of families of all kinds. Doppen and Hollstein, and then Kuo, explore in very different ways the role technology plays—both in terms of its potential danger as well as its ability to connect students in different countries and facilitate student interaction and participation in the global village.

The activities by Rahatzad, Sasser, Phillion, and Sharma; Fissel; Cushner; and Sakuda, each in their own way, aim to engage the student with others in real-life or simulated encounters to bridge difference and gain deeper understanding of the others' experiences. Finally, Ghosh and Raven each demonstrate how social-justice concerns can be developed through science education.

Section 2 presents eleven activities that address many underlying concepts that cut across and strongly influence educational process and that are commonly found in the social foundations. Whether it is gender, race, or socioeconomic status, challenges abound in our lives that provoke teachers to enhance equality in their work.

Among the many different contributions in this section, Hachey and Medina challenge us to critically examine gender and social class through two engaging exercises. The online activity presented by Osborne and Kriese addresses issues related to social class that are also the focus of a simulation activity by Caniglia. Understanding identity development and enhancing intercultural competence are addressed through a number of creative and engaging activities presented by Fitzgerald and Mattix, Gallavan, Clark, Vetter, Lara, and Fisette.

A comprehensive matrix of major disciplines and issues addressed by each of the activities can be found at the end of this Introduction in Table 1. Major attention is identified by • (= major attention) while minor attention is designated as ° (= minor attention).

In a *New York Times* article, Giorgio Gomelsky talked about his experience being a music producer and his philosophy about the role of music in our lives (Gonzalez, 2013). The reporter noted that Gomelsky touched on every subject, including the health of our planet, and the way that music could touch the soul and say something of importance.

The teacher who puts social justice at the forefront aspires to create a space where similar ideals are at work in the products that are created within a community. Our planet depends on healthy relationships between and among all the life forms that inhabit it. That is the message of the soul as it demonstrates its existence in our daily round on earth. That is the only important message that we can articulate with any confidence when we work with students and colleagues to achieve social justice ideals.

We hope you find value in this, and our companion volume.

—Kenneth Cushner and Joanne Kilgour Dowdy

REFERENCES

Cushner, K. (2011). Intercultural Research in Teacher Education: An Essential Intersection in the Preparation of Globally Competent Teachers. *Action in Teacher Education,* 33:5-6, 601–14.

Gonzalez, D. (2013). *New York Times,* April 19. Accessed June 4, 2013, from http://cityroom.blogs.nytimes.com/2013/04/19/his-studio-is-in-disrepair-but-his-passion-for-music-is-intact/.

McDonald, M., & Zeichner, K. (2009). Social justice teacher education. In W. Ayers, T. Quinn, & D. Stovall (Eds.), *Handbook of Social Justice in Education* (pp. 595–610). New York: Routledge.

Pittman, C. T. (2009). Multicultural education and social justice. *Intercultural Education,* 20 (2), 173–86.

Schoorman, D., & Bogotch, I. (2010). Moving beyond 'diversity' to 'social justice': The challenge to re-conceptualize multicultural education. *Intercultural Education,* 21(1), 79–85.

Activity Number

Discipline/Issue Addressed →

	A	B	C	D	E	F	G	H	I	J
1	•					°			•	
2	•			•						
3	•			•		°				
4	°			•				°		
5	•		°							
6	•						•		•	
7	•					•	•		•	
8	•									
9	•					°			•	
10	°								•	
11		°	•							
12			•		°					
13					•	°				
14					•	°				•
15							•			•
16		•						•		•
17						•				°
18	°					°		•	•	
19						•			•	
20						•			°	
21						•				
22	°					•				
23	°					•			•	

Table 1
Comprehensive Matrix of Activities and Discipline/Issue Addressed

Key

A = Social Studies   B = Math   • = major attention

C = Science   D = Early Childhood   ° = minor attention

E = Gender   F = Identity

G = Online   H = Field Experiences

I = Intercultural Competence   J = Socioeconomics

Table 1

Section 1

Addressing Social Justice through Social Studies and Science

"Ah, Richard"
Yours is the pretty poem,
(as befitting an inaugural,)
portraying an America
more in concert with the geography
of "This Land is Your Land,"
than with the separate songs
of people who do not lie under
the stitched together blanket
of your Kumbaya words.
What light you yield, what sights you point to
as you skip across our continental expanse.
You have found the voice, touched the hand,
recorded the sound of Working America,
but do not recognize our motley patchwork
thinly covers a country not whole.
There are gaping rents of sorrow,
loose threads of violence,
discolorations of disparities
that tear at our very fabric.
So Richard, sing your song of one America,
but remind yourself a dirge throbs below,
just under your ability to hear it.

—Mel Glenn

Activity 1

Futures Window

Kenneth Cushner

Pull a thread here and you'll find it's attached to the rest of the world.
—Nadeem Aslam, *The Wasted Vigil*

ABSTRACT

It is often a challenge for people, especially young students, to understand, identify with, and see the direct connection between their own lives and those of others—especially with those who live in places and in circumstances that are far removed from their own everyday existence and experience. Yet, as the world continues to shrink and people become increasingly interconnected, the very notion that our collective fate may be in jeopardy becomes increasingly essential to understand. In this exercise, students project into the future—both their own and that of the world at large—and consider how the two are interdependent.

BACKGROUND AND PURPOSE

Fundamental to the development of a global perspective is the notion of interconnectedness—an understanding that the human and natural environments are inextricably linked and that events that occur in one part of our global system have a direct or indirect influence on other elements of the system. Robert Hanvey (1976) referred to this as "knowledge of global dynamics," while Thomas Friedman (2006) referred to it as "the flat world." On the surface, this sounds easy to understand. But in reality, most people give little thought to how their own actions impact others or how the actions of others in other parts of the world may have a direct influence on their own future.

1

For more than twenty years, I have asked my students to consider how their own fate and future will be directly affected by what goes on elsewhere in the world. I ask my students to become futurists—that is, to read current trends that they see happening in their own lives and in those of others in the world and to predict how things may look in the future. They are not to generate a wish list but rather to base their predictions on what they see happening today and then projecting what this current activity might lead to in the future. Students do this first on their own, placing four or five entries into each quadrant, and then in small groups generate a group window. I then compile contributions from the class for all to view and consider.

LEARNING OBJECTIVES

As this activity unfolds, participants will:

- project what they think they will have accomplished or will be confronting in five and twenty years;
- project what they think will be confronting the world in five and twenty years; and
- reflect upon what they see happening in the world and how they think this will influence what they project for themselves.

PROCEDURE

1. Ask students to divide a page into quadrants, labeling the top half "The Self" and the bottom half "The World." The left side represents "5 years" while the right side represents "20 years."
2. Ask individuals to make at least five entries in each quadrant; things they expect to have accomplished or to be dealing with in five years and in twenty years, and things they expect the world will have accomplished or will be confronting in five as well as twenty years. (NOTE: Remind participants that they are not to record what they *wish* would happen, but what they *predict* will occur based on what they see happening today.)
3. When students seem to have stopped generating responses on their individual papers, have them contribute to a group version with classmates in their immediate vicinity.
4. Finally, generate a class version with you adding their examples on a flipchart or white board for all to see. A typical 'window' looks like this:

Self – 5 years	Self – 20 years
-graduated or being in graduate school	-graduate degree
-have a job	-moving into another career
-married	-traveling extensively
-own a home and car	-having children (or grandchildren)
-children	-paid off student loans
-taking that long-awaited vacation.	-having a vacation or second home
World – 5 years	World – 20 years
-more global disputes	-one world government
-the Middle East still in conflict	-population increase
-more energy shortages and more costly	-more frequent global conflicts
-increased unemployment and inflation	-ubiquitous use and dependence on technology
-continued growth in technology	-continued global climate change and greater
-increased global health concerns	environmental problems
-more pollution	-global more pandemics
	-greater dependence on new sources of energy

Figure 1.1. Futures Window

5. When contributions are visible for all to see, have individuals re-
    flect upon what they see. The following questions may be used as
    prompts:

    a) What messages seem to jump out at you as you look closely
       at the response patterns? (Do not be surprised if quick re-
       sponses do not emerge.) Encourage students to take some
       time to analyze the similarities as well as the differences in
       the columns. What generalizations seem to emerge? What
       questions do you have as a result of the generalizations you
       observed?

    b) As people analyze their responses, it is not uncommon to
       hear people say something like, "It seems as if things will be
       quite nice and easy for me while there are significant prob-
       lems in the world." This is a critical observation. If they have
       not already made this observation, encourage them to con-
       sider it.

    c) Let's assume that all can safely make this or a similar obser-
       vation, given the responses on the list. What is the respon-
       sibility one has to others? Why do you think it is that, in
       general, people project their own future to be fine even
       when the rest of the world continues to face problems and
       challenges?

    d) Next, look closely at your projections for the world. What
       generalizations stand out as you analyze this information? It
       is often said that each individual can and must do her or his
       own part to help improve the bigger picture. All of the prob-
       lems the world will face, whether they are in fact solved or
       not, will require the coordinated efforts of many different
       people from many different career and cultural back-
       grounds, who are able to work together. The problems of the
       world are such that they will be solved by the coordinated

efforts of many different people and nations, or they will not be solved at all.

e) What is the role of education in helping people develop the ability to solve the problems that you believe the world will face?

f) What are some things you can do through your teaching that will help your students develop the awareness, knowledge, and skills necessary to collaborate with others whose ways of interacting and values may be quite different from their own?

ADDITIONAL COMMENTS

The outcome of this exercise has not changed in more than two decades. When asked to step back and reflect upon their predictions, most students quickly see a surprising yet disturbing pattern emerge—their life is rosy and going as planned, while the rest of the world seems to be going to pot! Further discussion reveals that students typically do not feel connected to the rest of the world, nor do they understand the plight of others, reflecting an apparent disconnect between their own lives and how they might be impacted or affected by what is going on around them.

Students also fail to see that they are living in a world facing a wide array of problems that cross international borders and that will only be solved if people from many different cultures, speaking many different languages and holding many diverse beliefs, learn how to communicate, understand one another, become socially active, and collaborate; if not, they will not be solved. I challenge them to consider how they can be empowered to assume a social justice orientation—how they, along with their future students, can learn to take action to correct some wrongs and work to make the world a better place for all.

REFERENCES

Friedman, T. (2006). *The World Is Flat: A Brief History of the 21st Century*. New York: Farrar, Straus & Giroux.

Hanvey, R. (1976). *An Attainable Global Perspective*. New York: Center for Global Perspectives.

Activity 2

What Is a Family?

Martha Lash

ABSTRACT

Participants make representational drawings of their families at different ages, in approximately five-year increments from birth to the present day, including one projection five years into the future. These snapshots of who is included in the family over one's lifetime is a quick illustration of how the family of origin changes over time and can easily show who one considers to be part of the family in a quick, expressive, and fun manner. Through volunteer sharing of family drawings, "typical" families are shown to be diverse in number, composition, and explanation, causing participants to reexamine what it can mean to be a family.

BACKGROUND AND PURPOSE

A wide range of family structures exists in all communities and schools today (Children's Defense Fund, 2011; Trawick-Smith, 2010). It is imperative that teachers look beyond the definition of nuclear family, that is, a family with just a mother, father, and children living together, as this family structure makes up less than 25 percent of all families (US Census Bureau, 2010). It is time to recognize the integrity and worth of all children and their family makeups while simultaneously understanding children's and families' views of their own family. Supporting participants to understand and respect family diversity is an ideal starting place in their own growth and an authentic entry into children's worlds.

This activity is one tool to challenge participants' perspectives on a "typical" family, while educating individuals about the diversity of today's families and to affirm others' "family." First, a simple exercise allows participants to do a quick drawing of their family at various points in time, including a projection sometime in the future. Then, by sharing with other participants who have different family structures and who are also "typical," participants begin to realize that there is more to the notion of a "typical" family. This sets the stage for exploring multiple perspectives of "What is a family," by interpreting students' thinking from their own definition of family and encouraging seeing the perspectives of others.

LEARNING OBJECTIVES

Through a visual representation that employs self-reflection and a partnered/group sharing of findings, participants are prodded into perspective taking and redefining "typical" family. Participants will:

- learn to be visually expressive in a quick-print exercise of showing who they consider to be in their family at different times in their lives;
- learn how others define/depict a family;
- consider personalized and newfound perspectives of "what is family" as compared/contrasted to the government's definition of family; and
- collectively consider the composition of children's families currently (Children's Defense Fund, 2011; That's a Family!, 2000) and what is typical for children and how they might describe their family.

PROCESS

1. Ask participants to individually draw (in stick figures or symbols) "snapshots of their family membership" at various ages in their lives.
2. Have the participants draw who they consider to be in their family at birth, age 4, age 8, age 13, age 17, and "now"—their current age. Ask for one "projection" drawing of what they hope their family will look like in five years. Inform participants that they can include whomever/whatever they deem to be family in the drawing.
3. Invite participants to share with another person and/or in small groups. Ask participants to take turns describing and explaining their family drawings while others compare and contrast them to their own (i.e., who includes pets; grandparents living in and out of the house; stepsiblings; legal guardians; non-biologically related "family" living in the house?). Have participants share future family desires and note how some are alike and different.
4. As far as they are comfortable, have participants share with the entire group. Ask reflective questions: Whose family remains fairly

consistent over time? Whose changes? What happens to create change? Are some changes predictable? Do all of these depictions of each participant's family count at various times? What is the group's descriptive family?

ADDITIONAL COMMENTS

This activity can be revealing and generate discussion and introspection regarding what and who are considered "our family." The activity can be stopped at this point; however, it also lends itself to be extended in several ways, and in different sessions, depending on time. You might, for instance:

- Examine the Census Bureau's definition of family (US Census, 2010). "Family: A family is a group of two people or more (one of whom is the householder) related by birth, marriage, or adoption and residing together; all such people (including related subfamily members) are considered as members of one family." How does that definition compare to the participants' definitions as depicted? What does it mean to be a "subfamily" member? Ask participants if they used/considered the term "subfamily member" when drawing their family and/or when they talk about their family members.
- Collectively consider how children's families today are composed (Children's Defense Fund, 2011; That's a Family!, 2000). Is there a typical family? If so, what might it look like? If not, offer suggestions of some of the more common family structures that exist in today's society. How would they play out in activities that you might do on families in classrooms?
- What does it mean to be a "family-oriented" school/program? Would all of the depicted families in the drawings be welcomed? What about families that were not generated by the drawings? Are schools/programs prepared to welcome all families? What types of considerations would schools/programs need to incorporate to be family oriented? Review resources (i.e., Copple, 2003; National Association for the Education of Young Children, n.d.; Turner-Vorbeck & Miller Marsh, 2008); consider the merits of each.
- Look at programs that offer "family" memberships. Who do they consider to make up a family? Are there considerations for how many people are to be included in the family, or are there simply "family rates"? Is this fair to small families? Large families? Does the program state legal parameters for determining family? Do those parameters seem fair and reflective of all families?
- Consider communications that are sent to the "family" of the children in schools. What are the best salutations for addressing families and/or legal guardians? Consider children in a wide range of

families and how they might prefer that letters going to their family be addressed.

- Consider how families are depicted in popular culture, particularly television and movies. How have television and movies portrayed families over time? Have those depictions been reflective of the broader culture at that time? Have certain family structures been romanticized? (Coontz, 1992). Have certain family structures been forgotten? Are certain family structures more easily depicted in comedies, love stories, or dramas?

Sample drawings are in figures 2.1 through 2.4.

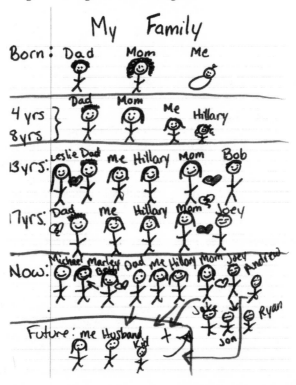

Figure 2.1.

In this student's drawing, we see that she was the firstborn of two daughters to her biological parents, and that somewhere between the ages of 8 and 13 (or second and seventh grade) her parents divorced and were each in relationships with others which she symbolizes with a heart. At 17, the student still shows one sister and that each of her parents has a "broken heart," and her mother has a new relationship with a full heart.

Between the ages of 17 and the present (24 for this student), she shows an expanded family with her sister still present; Dad is in a new relationship with someone who had a child and their new relationship has given her this stepbrother as well as a half sibling. Mom's new spouse brings in two stepbrothers and we learn that she has two half brothers from their union. Interestingly, she sees herself married with children in five years, and the arrow she draws of who will also be part of her family, includes her dad, mom, and sister, who lived together at least the first eight years of her life.

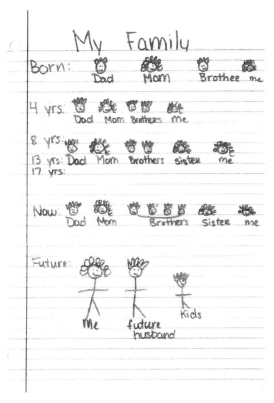

Figure 2.2.

In this family drawing (figure 2.2), the student's family looks fairly stable with parents and siblings. However, as it turned out, the student described remarriages and stepbrothers, but only reflected the family that was living in the house at the time.

Figure 2.3a

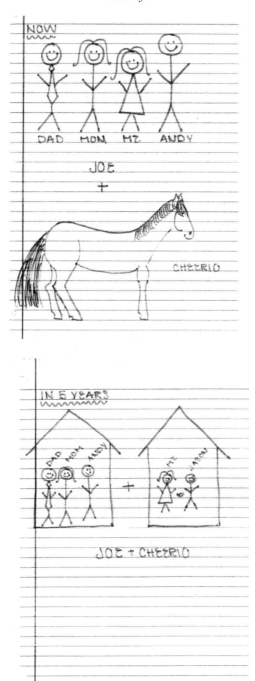

Figure 2.3b

In this student's drawings above we see the importance of having a horse from the age of four onward, including sharing horses after she is married. While many students put cats and dogs in the drawings, occasionally there is the unexpected horse, or in the case of one male student, a Volkswagen Beetle—one at age 5, another added at age 13, and another planned for five years in the future; he stated that receiving and working on these cars with his father made the cars seem like part of the family. In other drawings, it is not uncommon to see grandparents or extended family members.

REFERENCES

Children's Defense Fund. (2011). *State of America's Children 2011 Report*. Washington, DC: Author.

Coontz, S. (1992). *The Way We Never Were: American Families and the Nostalgia Trap*. New York: Basic Books.

Copple, C. (Ed.). (2003). *A World of Difference: Readings on Teaching Young Children in a Diverse Society*. Washington, DC: NAEYC.

National Association for the Education of Young Children: Engaging Diverse Families. (n.d.). Retrieved from http://www.naeyc.org/familyengagement.

That's a Family!: A Film for Kids About Family Diversity. (2000). Respect for All Project (DVD). San Francisco: Groundspark.

Trawick-Smith, J. (2010). *Early Childhood Development: A Multicultural Perspective* (5th ed.). Columbus, OH: Merrill.

Turner-Vorbeck, T., & Miller Marsh, M. (2008). *Other Kinds of Families: Embracing Diversity in Schools*. New York: Teacher College Press.

US Census Bureau of Household and Family Statistics. (2010). Washington, DC. Retrieved from http://www.census.gov/population/www.cps/cpsdef.htm.

Activity 3

Ideal Types and Transgressors: Reinterpreting the "Family Tree" Experience

Janice Kroeger

ABSTRACT

The family tree activity is one experience that elementary teachers often choose as a language and literacy activity or as a social studies and community building activity in the classroom without critically reflecting upon the activities' merits or downfalls. In my own growing-up years, I remember sitting in elementary, junior high, and even high school social studies classrooms and often being asked, "Who are the important people in your family? How are they related to you? Why are they special? Where did they come from?"

While many students might experience this request in a "non-threatening" manner—and even university pre-service teachers experience this with openness and optimism—others would likely react with a knee-jerk reaction of caution and dismay because of their own personal "back stories." Such activities might open up some "transgressive" boundaries that are known to the student but are more challenging to disclose in a group of like-aged peers.

I raise the primary point here that when students are asked to sketch and label genealogical histories within their family utilizing a tree as a metaphor, the family tree itself becomes a binding trap that often denies the existence of family ties that are transgressive, different from the mainstream, troubled, strong in unique ways, non-biologically bound, and/or outside of the realm of socially polite conversation. I am not suggesting that teachers avoid discussions within groups that allow children to authentically share their varied and complex lives, but rather, by posing some relevant questions about the variety of types of families that exist and how children might experience this common classroom activity, we can more carefully construct relevant opportunities.

In making this suggestion, I draw from a reading in the book *Other Kinds of Families: Embracing Diversity in Schools* (Turner-Vorbeck & Miller Marsh, 2008) and recreate a simple icebreaking experience that I commonly do with pre-service teachers in the university classroom. In doing this work, I ask them to "deconstruct" their own notions of "normal family" by using an introductory chapter entitled "Hegemonies and Transgressions of Family: Tales of Pride and Prejudice" (Heilman, 2008, pp. 7–27).

In recreating this common childhood experience with pre-service teachers, I've come to believe one result of the "family tree" experience that young students face may be to "cover" for their family, feel uncomfortable, act as if their family is more like everyone else's, or come to see the realities of their family life beyond the bounds of a "normal" or ideal type, thus marginalizing them further from their own rightful place in the classroom community. With my students, I question a teacher's role in this activity, thus arguing for adjustments, caveats, and more appropriate social practices in classrooms today.

BACKGROUND AND PURPOSE

Because many elementary teachers replicate popular experiences they've encountered in schools without critically examining the implications of those experiences on their students, it is important to "deconstruct" experiences like the family tree exercise. When enacting the sketching of a family tree—with a trunk, ensuring branches, twigs, leaves, and stems and labeling them with important families ties, names, and roles associated with those ties—we must examine how many children or students will likely experience this activity with dread and shame because what they have does not match what Heilman (2008) calls the "normal and ideal" type (pp. 7–9).

LEARNING OBJECTIVES

I ask the pre-service teachers to engage in the following seven steps and ask the following questions:

Figure 3.1.

1. Read Heilman's chapter in the edited book by Taylor-Vorbeck and Miller Marsh and attempt to understand the following terms:

   - Hegemony
   - Normal
   - Ideal family
   - Socially constructed family
   - The family we live "by"
   - Negative self-judgment
   - Family size and composition
   - Homogeneity among members
   - Stigma and prejudice
   - Social stress
   - Family transgressors

2. As you are creating your family tree, pay attention not to the "ideal type" that your family is, but to the "transgressive" elements of size, composition, religious expression, marital status, race, sexuality, social class, and ethnicity (or other complexities) that are present.

3. If you were to assign this activity (without the transgressive element) to a group of typical K–3 students, how would they be likely to perform?
4. What elements of your family tree would be difficult for them to disclose among their peers? Among teachers?
5. In what situations would this activity be acceptable to you as a critical teacher educator?
6. What would you do to adapt this experience for children?
7. Is a family tree assignment appropriate? Why or why not?

OUTCOMES OF THIS PROCESS

As I ask university students to read the chapter "Hegemonies and Transgressions of Family: Tales of Pride and Prejudice" by Heilman (2008) and they define the terms the author uses, in their own words students begin to recognize how society promotes a particular type of ideal heterosexual, two-parent couple as the norm; yet many of them and I acknowledge the various forms of marriage (or lack of) in their own lives. As participants attempt to use a provided sketch of a "tree" and map their own biological or found parents, siblings, and/or sibling and parental marriage partners onto the family tree, we discuss which relationships are difficult to convey.

Often, students whose parents have experienced divorce, remarriage(s), or multiple legally unsanctioned relationships, confess their lack of comfort at describing or reconciling the ways their parents' marriage partners have shaped their own identities in families. Students who've severed ties with parents or siblings or have experienced challenges in being parented by their biological kin, but have had other types of parenting, reveal themselves. Including stepbrothers, stepsisters, and stepparents adds another complex dimension to this experience, raising questions of how to "diagram" various members onto limbs or branches.

Thus I often ask the question, "How might an alternative symbol to a 'tree' provide a better metaphor than the tree allows?" Some students create a "forest" or "bush" instead of a tree; others create roots beneath the soil to convey complex family histories; still others add extra limbs and branches to their trees or create cracks in their branches when marriages and sibling relationships or other family changes create dysfunction or disharmonies in families.

I instruct participants to identify any "ideal" family relationships within their own family tree as well as any "transgressors" that may be present in their own family history but not apparent at first glance (e.g., illegitimate births; adoptive or fostered family members, as well as family members without biological or marriage ties; gay, lesbian, transgendered, or queer members; members who have significant challenges such as incarceration, drug or alcohol problems, or mental health challenges). I then ask students to reflect on which relationships in their students' families are likely to be celebrated and which are likely to be downplayed by children, and why.

After this heavy-hitting question, I find that it is only then that the family tree experience begins to be an "authentic" classroom-community-building experience because it allows students to reflect upon some of their unique or shared struggles to reconcile the complexity of daily life in families. When transgressive elements are added to the family tree experience, students disclose an array of challenging aspects of family life—such as a parent losing a job, experiencing divorce, and being on welfare (or living with extended family), having a gay parent coming out in middle age, or having a family member in prison or living in a shelter.

All of these opportunities for discussion that are part of the daily fabric of human complexity bring us closer as a community. Most students recognize how much trust they have to feel for their classmates to discuss such matters and empathize greatly with students in their classrooms who have similar lenses with which they view family experiences. They begin to notice how schools are structured, and reflect that children may not have the ability or opportunity to articulate their life experiences, and yet may need such rich daily experiences to gain mastery over the complexity that their lives bring. At this point many pre-service teachers reject the family tree activity in favor of more appropriate experiences for all children.

At the end of this icebreaker, we discuss the ramifications of the project for young children (kindergarten) and for children across the primary grades (first, second, and third grade and beyond). They begin to recognize the variety of children in schools whose life experiences would never allow them to fully find comfort in the classroom in this activity or whose life experiences would likely lead to "covering" or being fully "silenced" by the family tree activity (especially over years in schools).

We then discuss what adjustments it would take for children to find appropriate comfort in our classroom. Often, students discover they themselves were that child for whom teachers made adjustments that allowed them to acknowledge their "transgressive" family life without feeling or being singled out in a marginalizing way. Pre-service teachers also think about the children in their own classrooms and the appropriate adjustments to make in light of what they've learned by deconstructing the "family tree."

REFERENCES

Heilman, E. (2008). Hegemonies and "transgressions" of family: Tales of pride and prejudice. (Eds. T. Turner-Vorbeck, & M. Miller Marsh). In, *Other kinds of families: Embracing diversity in schools* (pp. 7–17). New York, Teacher College Press.

Turner-Vorbeck, T. & M. Miller Marsh (2008). *Other kinds of families: Embracing diversity in schools.* New York, Teacher College Press.

Activity 4

Do You See What I See?: Using Critical Role-Play to Help Prospective Teachers View Activities from Multiple Perspectives

Monica Miller Marsh

ABSTRACT

Critical role-play can be used to help prospective teachers see the effect their lessons and activities have on the children and families in their care (Shapiro & Leopold, 2012). In this particular lesson, prospective teachers plan and implement an introductory activity that they have designed to be inclusive of all children and families, and also take on the roles of children and family members or guardians as they participate in the activities created and taught by their peers. Prospective teachers then reflect upon the activities from multiple perspectives and collaboratively work to revise them so that children and families from every background are made visible in their classrooms.

BACKGROUND AND PURPOSE

While much is written about utilizing role-play for educative purposes across a variety of disciplines (Graff, 2012; Jenkins & Turick-Gibson, 1999; Poorman, 2002; Schaap, 2005), there is no common definition of role-play. When I use the term "role-play," I am referring to *critical role-play* as defined by Shapiro and Leopold (2012). According to Shapiro and Leopold,

> Critical role-play requires students to embody voices and perspectives that may be quite different from their own. It asks them to speak and write using discourse that may be unfamiliar. It encourages them to explore relationships among people, texts, and contexts. (p. 123)

19

The act of being engaged in critical role-play means that prospective teachers are positioned in ways that encourage emotional as well as cognitive responses. In this particular assignment, prospective teachers have the opportunity to view the activity through the eyes of the teacher, the eyes of a family member or guardian, and the eyes of the child. In addition, they are often responding to the activity from a cultural, linguistic, sexual, or economic perspective that is very different from their own. In many cases, those who are used to being "seen" in the classroom experience the frustration of being invisible.

For this assignment, prospective teachers are asked to design an activity to be used at a Meet the Parent Night (Pushor, 2008) that would help them to learn more about the children and families in their care. Since the intent is for every family to participate in the activity, participants are asked to take into account the composition of all families including differences in family structure (children who are adopted, in foster care, being raised by grandparents, etc.), race/ethnicity, socioeconomic status, sexual orientation, culture, language, and physical and cognitive abilities. Participants then present their activities to their peers who are placed in the roles of the children and families or guardians who might comprise their future classrooms.

LEARNING OBJECTIVES

Participants will:

- develop an activity that can be used with all families during a Meet the Parent Night;
- present the activity to their peers who have been asked to role-play the children and families or guardians who will be in attendance;
- collaboratively debrief and reflect upon the activity, providing opportunities for all voices to be heard; and
- discuss how the activity can be revised so that children and families who were excluded during the role-play will become a part of the classroom community.

PROCESS

1. Participants are asked to read Debbie Pushor's (2008) chapter, "Are Schools Doing Enough to Learn About Families?" In this chapter, Pushor, a Canadian educator and advocate for families, asked us to imagine a Meet the Parent Night where children and families have an opportunity to share their stories with one another and help define the expectations for school. This runs contrary to the traditional Meet the Teacher Night or Curriculum Night where the

teacher shares the stories and defines the expectations of, and for, families.

2. Participants are then directed to create a Meet the Parent Night activity that will take into account the composition of all families, including differences in race, ethnicity, socioeconomic status, sexual orientation, culture, language, religion, and physical and cognitive abilities. In other words, the objective is to create an inclusive activity in which all family members are able to participate.

3. The Meet the Parent Night activities are then presented to peers who have all been given roles to assume as parents in the classroom. These roles shift for every activity. For example, some class members are given cards that specify they are non-English speakers, or that they cannot read, or that they are wheelchair-bound. The next activity may consist of a group of parents and guardians that includes equal numbers of parents who would be considered in poverty, a lesbian family, and a family who identifies as fundamentalist Christian.

4. After the activity is completed, the entire class is debriefed. Participants who were placed in the role of family members discuss how it felt to be part of an activity in which they were or were not able to participate, for example, because of not being able to speak English in order to participate in the activity or being someone in poverty asked to share stories about their summer vacation.

5. Participants work collaboratively to revise the activities to be more inclusive.

ADDITIONAL COMMENTS

There are many occasions in this exercise when students were positioned in ways that rendered them invisible. During one activity, two students who were positioned as non-English speakers became frustrated. After fifteen minutes of not being seen or heard they decided to sit out, determining that for them this activity was a "waste of time." During the next activity, students who were positioned as being in poverty admitted to not being truthful about their answers in order to participate in an activity that asked them to talk about their favorite restaurant and where they had spent their summer vacation. We related these responses to how real families and children must feel when positioned in similar ways.

As we all worked toward making spaces for authentic family stories to be told, activities shifted from being structured, highly biased, and language-based, to activities that allowed families to interact with one another and to share information in a more natural, relaxed manner. The types of activities that proved to be most inclusive were those that allowed children and families to interact through images, such as creating and sharing family collages created from magazines and other printed materials, and those that engaged all families in working together toward a common goal, such as preparing and then eating a fruit salad.

Prospective teachers came to the realization that these types of encounters between teachers and families need to occur on a continual basis if we truly desire all families to be seen and heard in our classrooms.

REFERENCES

Graff, R. (2012). Role-play in clinical research training: Rationale and guide for exercises. Unpublished Master's Thesis. Northwestern University. Evanston, IL.

Jenkins, P., & Turick-Gibson, T. (1999). An exercise in critical thinking using role playing. *Nurse Educator, 24*(6), 11–14.

Poorman, P. B. (2002). Biography and role-playing: Fostering empathy in abnormal psychology. *Teaching of Psychology, 29*(1), 32–36.

Pushor, D. (2008). Are schools doing enough to learn about families? In T. Turner-Vorbeck & M. Miller Marsh (Eds.), *Learning to Listen to Families in Schools*. New York: Teachers College Press.

Schaap, A. (2005). Learning political theory by role-playing. *Politics, 25*(1), 46–52.

Shapiro, S., & Leopold, L. (2012). A critical role for role-playing pedagogy. *TESL Canada Journal, 29*(2), 120–30.

Activity 5

From Chernobyl to Fukushima: Teaching for Global Justice

Frans H. Doppen and Matthew S. Hollstein

ABSTRACT

This activity presents a sequence of three lesson activities focused on the transformation of nuclear power as a weapon of war into a source of electrical energy marked by periodic disasters. We recommend that teachers allocate approximately one week to each activity. In the first activity the teacher presents historical background information and engages students in exploring and presenting multiple perspectives on the use of nuclear energy. In the second activity students learn about the human responses that have followed a nuclear disaster and vocalize their thoughts through readers' theater. The third activity engages students in a Socratic seminar to debate the future of nuclear energy.

BACKGROUND AND PURPOSE

One month after Hurricane Sandy slammed the East Coast of the United States causing massive damage, disrupting and destroying communities as well as posing a potential threat to coastal nuclear power plants (such as at Oyster Creek in New Jersey), Atlanta-based Southern Company spokesperson Cheri Collins claimed, "We learned a lot from Fukushima, and all that has been taken into account." She explained the two planned nuclear reactors at Plant Vogtle in Waynesboro, Georgia, will feature safety devices to prevent another nuclear disaster such as at Fukushima (Rand, 2012).

The two new Vogtle reactors, scheduled to be completed in 2016 and 2017, are the first reactors to be approved since the year before the Three Mile Island nuclear meltdown, which occurred on March 28, 1979. Since then, the world has witnessed two other nuclear disasters, one at Cherno-byl, Ukraine (then in the USSR), on April 26, 1986, and one at Fukushima, Japan, on March 11, 2011 (Rand, 2012). Reactions after Fukushima have differed around the world, from continuing construction (United States, Netherlands, South Korea) to calling off plans to start building new plants (Italy) to completely closing all down (Belgium, Germany) (The Implications of Fukushima, 2011).

Quoting Hannah Arendt that, "education is the point at which we decide whether we love the world enough to assume responsibility for it," Graham Pike (2012) recently suggested that we live in a time of dis-comfort that calls for creating active global citizens. Reminding us of Albert Camus' notion that great ideas "come into the world as gently as doves," he calls upon teachers to help students widen their circle of com-passion to embrace all living creatures and the whole of nature on our global planet and to educate students for sustainable development.

Preparing future global citizens to care about all living things as well as the human-made world is characterized by a perennial struggle be-tween the progress science has to offer and the human response it engen-ders (Noddings, 1992). In a Western world, characterized by a ruptured relationship between mind and nature (Bai & Scutt, 2009), citizens often lack the power and resources to make their voices heard and are often dismissed as emotional and reactive (Fleury & Sheldon, 1996). Yet, as global educators it is our mission to "help young people to make in-formed and reasoned decisions for the public good . . . in an interdepen-dent world" (National Council for the Social Studies, 2010).

Engaging students in perspective taking is crucial in helping them develop their own personal perspectives. While perspective taking may include emotional dimensions, it does not involve imagination. Instead it involves well-grounded but tentative conclusions based on a deep under-standing of why people did what they did, an appreciation of the context in which they found themselves, and multiple competing forms of evi-dence (Davis, 2001; Foster, 2001; Wineburg & Wilson, 2001).

These activities are designed to raise students' awareness of the use of nuclear energy as a global social-justice issue that transcends national boundaries and calls for intercultural understanding. They also provide good models of readers' theater and Socratic seminar strategies. Readers' theater is an engaging strategy that allows teachers to diverge from teach-er-centered instruction and allows students who struggle in other areas to excel by performing for an audience.

Readers' theater is an effective way to bring to the surface voices that are usually not heard (Cruz & Murthy, 2006; Maher, 2006; Romano & Glascock, 2002). It actively engages students in subject matter and pro-vides them with an opportunity to write (McKay, 1997). Finally, through dramatic reading, readers' theater helps students gain a deeper understanding and make connections with the time and place of the character they perform (Morris, 2003).

While teachers may often wonder whether discussion in the classroom is worth the trouble, especially when it involves a controversial issue, when it is well planned and adequately prepared for it is an effective method to engage students in developing new personal perspectives (Hess, 2004).

A Socratic seminar is an exploratory intellectual instruction-through-questioning conversation (Chorzempa & Lapidus, 2009). It engages students in authentic discussion and avoids bull sessions by framing an essential question designed to seek a deeper understanding of complex issues and events through rigorously informed dialogue (Eisen, 2007; Kohlmeier, 2006; Ludy & Plumb, 2000). An effective seminar also teaches students how to listen across differences while disagreeing civilly with each other. It helps them to develop useful negotiation skills and skill in using reasoned arguments and persuasive evidence. Ultimately, Socratic seminars enable students to better grasp human nature and develop a personal voice (Chorzempa & Lapidus, 2009; North, 2009).

LEARNING OUTCOMES FOR ACTIVITY 1: HISTORICAL BACKGROUND

Activity 1 is an important introduction as it provides a foundation of knowledge students will need for activities 2 and 3. It is designed to:

- inform and engage students through documentary films, traditional lecture, and individual research projects to develop a historical understanding of the development of nuclear technology and the disasters at Chernobyl and Fukushima; and
- facilitate an understanding of how significant nuclear events have elicited different responses given their unique temporal and cultural context.

Nuclear power has had a dramatic and tumultuous history, from its origin as a weapon of war with the Manhattan project to its more peaceful, yet potentially destructive, role as a source of civilian power (Doppen, 2000). Deemed to be the solution to the world's energy problems in the early 1960s, today many still weigh its benefits against the potential devastation it may bring.

Several excellent documentaries on the Manhattan Project, Chernobyl, and Fukushima are available on the Internet and can be downloaded for free (see Resources). While each documentary provides a historical overview, each one also helps students to examine its topic's impact across different cultures.

Using authentic footage, *The Atomic Café* documents the development of the atomic bomb by the Manhattan project and subsequent developments during the Cold War. *The Battle for Chernobyl* vividly depicts the devastating power of nuclear energy when management fails. PBS's *Frontline* documentary *Inside Japan's Nuclear Meltdown* examines the meltdown of Tokyo Electric Power Company's (TEPCO) Fukushima Daiichi nuclear reactor. Each documentary features contemporary faces and voices of individuals who were directly impacted by the experience.

After having watched each documentary, in its entirety or through selected segments, students should have gained an initial appreciation of how cultural context elicited similar, as well as dissimilar, responses. To follow up, the teacher then should help students to organize these responses, for example, through a Venn diagram. Each documentary can also be supplemented with focused lectures that detail the transition of nuclear technology from military to civilian use and provide a context for each event with respect to its global, regional, and local geographic location.

Teachers should begin discussions with students regarding the desultory responses to the Chernobyl and Fukushima-Daiichi nuclear disasters. This is an important question, given the nature of the two disasters. Ask students whether or not the operators of these facilities fully understood the awesome power and responsibility they were in charge of and whether these two disasters could have been prevented. These questions will help to elicit conversations about social equity, fairness, and social/moral responsibility surrounding the use of nuclear power.

As a follow-up activity teachers might ask their students to conduct an individual or group research project to examine Soviet and Japanese newspapers published in English. The students should examine how Chernobyl and Fukushima were reported, how the Soviet and Japanese governments responded, and whether the newspapers accurately reported the disaster. This will allow students to consider issues of social justice, most notably in terms of those who were affected during the aftermaths. Examining how the USSR and Japan each responded to tragedy, especially in comparison to the American response to the meltdown at Three Mile Island, can do much to foster students' intercultural understandings.

LEARNING OUTCOMES FOR ACTIVITY 2: READER'S THEATER

The meltdowns at Chernobyl and Fukushima were caused by human error and natural disaster respectively (Friedman, 2011). These two events exemplify the awesome power of nuclear energy and, more importantly, showcase the devastation that it can bring when things go wrong. Although students are often asked to read historical accounts of major historical events, much of what they read fails to adequately convey the human experience (Cruz & Murthy, 2006). The purpose of this activity is: Facilitate students' abilities to make a personal connection and gain a deeper intercultural understanding of nuclear events through firsthand accounts of survivors.

Readers' theater enables teachers to use authentic voices to present multiple historical perspectives (Cruz & Murphy, 2006; Davis, 2001; Foster, 2001). To prepare for a successful readers' theater, students may benefit from either live examples or videos of others performing readers' theater. Many of these videos can be searched for on the Internet and accessed for free on such websites as YouTube.

Voices from Chernobyl: The Oral History of a Nuclear Disaster (Alexievich, 2006) provides students with powerful personal accounts. The website for *Fukushima: Inside Japan's Nuclear Meltdown* (PBS, 2012) includes several links to first-hand accounts as well. To ensure multiple voices are included in the performance, individual students should be assigned specific roles. However, allowing them to select their own passages will empower them to develop a personal connection to the text. As a final step they will be expected to perform their selections (Morris, 2003; Reading Rockets, 2013; Vermilion Parish Schools, 2010).

In a social studies methods course at the collegiate level as well as in a secondary social studies classroom, we found that readers' theater was very well received. Both the pre-service teachers and students commented on how this experience enhanced their learning. Two pre-service teachers commented that "the reading gave a voice to the people that experienced this horrific tragedy" and that "first person accounts give a voice to an event in history as opposed to a dry textbook with only facts on the subject."

Engaging in readers' theater also enhanced the pre-service teachers' appreciation of how they might use this activity someday in their own classrooms, as it gave them a personal understanding of the exercise from the perspective of the student. The high school students who participated in the readers' theater offered responses that suggested an enhanced empathy for those who experienced these tragedies. For example, while Elijah wrote that, "It was very sad and made me realize that some people were preparing to die or were dying," Christy stated that, "Hearing the real stories changed how I view the events; it wasn't history, it was real."

These responses exemplify how readers' theater dramatically enhances students' experiences. Readers' theater and other simulation activities humanize what really happened at Chernobyl and Fukushima and allows teachers to begin to address issues of social justice and intercultural awareness.

LEARNING OUTCOMES FOR ACTIVITY 3: THE SOCRATIC SEMINAR

Activity 3 seeks to:

- foster in students the ability to examine the controversy surrounding the use of nuclear energy in the structured intellectual debate format of a Socratic seminar; and,
- following a debriefing, the lesson culminates in a reflective writing exercise in which each student articulates his or her personal perspective on the use of nuclear power.

The Socratic seminar provides an excellent avenue for critically examining controversial issues, a realm many teachers seek to avoid. However, when adequately planned, it provides a powerful opportunity to engage students and help them clarify their personal perspectives (Hess, 2004). An effective seminar is student driven rather than teacher led. However, it is important that the teacher frame the controversy through a thoughtful and provocative central question.

Framing an effective central question will actively engage students in an intellectual conversation that truly examines the key issues that frame the controversy rather than its minutiae (Alfonsi, 2008). A sample question might be, "Given its potential destructive consequences, should we continue the global use of nuclear energy? Be specific and cite historical details to support your argument." As in Activity 2, the teacher may wish to assign specific roles during the seminar to remind the students of the multiple perspectives that frame the issue. During the seminar, the students should be encouraged to keep notes of the major points that are raised.

Upon conclusion of the seminar the students will have been engaged in an in-depth intellectual conversation that should have brought to the surface answers but also raised new questions (Alfonsi, 2008). This will provide a unique opportunity to debrief the experience through a whole-class dialogue allowing the teacher to frame guidelines for a final reflective written essay in which each student synthesizes what he or she has learned in a personal perspective on the use of nuclear energy.

ADDITIONAL COMMENTS

In this chapter we have presented three separate lesson activities. When combined, they foster an increased awareness of the inequitable impact on those affected by nuclear disaster. It also helps students to develop an understanding of the cultural context of the global use of nuclear energy. By examining the historical use of nuclear energy, developing empathy through readers' theaters, and engaging in Socratic dialogue, students begin to appreciate the impact of nuclear disaster on all citizens of our planet.

The development and use of nuclear weapons and the evolution to the civilian use of nuclear power has been filled with catastrophic events. Often those who have been least able to deal with these disasters have been most directly impacted. Ensuring that students understand the broad and far-reaching implications of the use and potential disaster associated with nuclear power is essential to fostering dialogue for potential change.

Issues of social justice and inequity are at the heart of the lesson activities we have suggested. It is our responsibility as teacher educators and teachers to help our students learn to make informed decisions through real-life examples and simulations that foster increased awareness and a deeper understanding of the great responsibility that will be passed on to future generations. The use of nuclear energy is not something that can be changed or removed overnight.

To effect real and lasting change will take the efforts of teacher educators, teachers, and students alike to be and become citizens who are informed by factual knowledge about the use of nuclear power and also have an affective appreciation of its awesome power. We believe that the lesson activities we have suggested in this chapter will not only encourage our students but will also encourage teacher educators and teachers to develop the necessary knowledge and intercultural empathy to be a voice for global justice.

RESOURCES

The Atomic Bomb

Rafferty, K., Loader, J., & Rafferty, P. (2002). (Directors). *The atomic café*. New Video Group, Inc. Retrieved from http://topdocumentaryfilms.com/the-atomic-cafe/.

Three Mile Island

PBS. (1999). *The American experience: Meltdown at Three Mile Island*. Retrieved from http://www.youtube.com/view_play_list?annotation_id=annotation_358537&feature=iv&p=937B0E873F58A3D7&src_vid=eLPAigMuBk0 .

Chernobyl

Alexievich, S. (2006). Voices from Chernobyl: *The Oral History of a Nuclear Disaster*. New York: Picador.

Johnson, T. (Director). *The Battle of Chernobyl*. (2006). Retrieved from http://topdocumentaryfilms.com/the-battle-of-chernobyl/.

Fukushima

PBS. (2012). *Frontline: Inside Japan's Nuclear Meltdown.* Retrieved from http://www.pbs.org/wgbh/pages/frontline/japans-nuclear-melt-down/.

Readers' Theater

Reading Rockets. (2013). Classroom strategies: Reader's theater. Retrieved from http://www.readingrockets.org/strategies/readers_theater/.

Vermillion Parish Schools. (2010). Vermillion Parish reader's theater. Retrieved from http://www.vrml.k12.la.us/curriculum/reader_theatre/home.htm.

REFERENCES

Alfonsi, C. (2008). Hey, teacher! Get off that stage: Assessing student thinking with Socratic seminars. *Ohio Journal of English Language Arts,* 48(1), 65–71.

Bai, H., & Scutt, G. (2009). Touching the earth with the heart of an enlightened mind: The Buddhist practice of mindfulness for environmental education. *Canadian Journal of Environmental Education,* 14, 92–106.

Chorzempa, B. F., & Lapidus, L. (2009). To find yourself, think for yourself. *Teaching Exceptional Children,* 41(3), 54–59.

Cruz, B. C., & Murthy, S. A. (2006). Breathing life into history: Using role-playing to engage students. *Social Studies and the Young Learner,* 19(1), 4–8.

Davis, O. L., Jr. (2001). In pursuit of historical empathy. In O. L. Davis, E. A. Yeager, & S. J. Foster (Eds.), *Historical Empathy and Perspective Taking in the Social Studies.* (pp. 1–2) Lanham, MD: Rowman & Littlefield Publishers, Inc.

Doppen, F. H. (2000). Teaching and learning multiple perspectives: The atomic bomb. *The Social Studies,* 91, 159–69.

Eisen, P. S. (2007). Yo Socrates: Amend this! *School Library Media Activities,* 24(2), 18–21.

Fleury, S. C., & Sheldon, A. (1996). Environmentalism and environmental issues. In R. W. Evans and D. W. Saxe (Eds.), *Handbook on Teaching Social Issues* (pp. 188–96) Washington, DC: National Council for the Social Studies.

Foster, S. J. (2001). Historical empathy in theory and practice: Some final thoughts. In O. L. Davis, E. A. Yeager, & S. J. Foster (Eds.), *Historical Empathy and Perspective Taking in the Social Studies.* (pp. 167–81) Lanham, MD: Rowman & Littlefield Publishers, Inc.

Friedman, S. M. (2011). Three Mile Island, Chernobyl, and Fukushima: An analysis of traditional and new media coverage of nuclear accidents and radiation. *Bulletin of the Atomic Scientists,* 67(5), 55–65.

Hess, D. (2004). Discussion in social studies: Is it worth the trouble? *Social Education,* 68(2), 151–55.

The Implications of Fukushima. (2011). *Bulletin of the Atomic Scientists,* 67(4), 8–22. doi: 10.117/009634021141480.

Kohlmeier, J. (2006). "Couldn't she just leave?" The relationship between consistently using class discussions and the development of historical empathy in a 9th grade World History course. *Theory and Research in Social Education,* 34(1), 34–57.

Ludy, J., & Plumb, B. (2000). Immersion circles and the Socratic seminar process. *California English,* 6(2), 26–27.

Maher, J. (2006). *Most Dangerous Women: Bringing History to Life through Readers' Theater.* Portsmouth, NH: Heinemann.

McKay, R. (1997). Essential ways of knowing drama and the visual arts in social studies: Current concerns. *Canadian Social Studies*, 31(3), 116.

Morris, R. (2003). Acting out history: Students reach across time and space. *International Journal of Social Education*, 18(1), 44–51.

National Council for the Social Studies. (2010). *National curriculum standards for social studies: A framework for teaching, learning, and assessment*. Silver Spring, MA: Author.

Noddings, N. (1992). *The Challenge to Care in Schools: An Alternative Approach to Education*. New York: Teachers College Press.

North, C. (2009). The promise and peril of developing democratic literacy for social justice. *Curriculum Inquiry*, 39(4), 555–79.

Pike, G. (2012, November). Global education in times of discomfort. Jan L. Tucker Memorial Lecture at the annual meeting of the International Assembly of the National Council for the Social Studies, Seattle, WA.

Rand, M. (December 3, 2012). Fukushima inspires safety features for Georgia nuclear reactors. CNN. Retrieved from http://www.cnn.com/2012/12/01/us/fukushima-safety-measures/index.html.

Romano, R. M., & Glascock, C. H. (2002). *Hungry Minds in Hard Times: Educating for Complexity for Students in Poverty*. New York: Peter Lang.

Wineburg, S., & Wilson, S. M. (2001). Peering at history through different lenses. In S. Wineburg (Ed.), *Historical Thinking and Other Unnatural Acts: Charting the Future of Teaching the Past* (pp. 139–54) Philadelphia, PA: Temple University Press.

Activity 6

Global Learning Wiki

Chia-Ling Kuo

ABSTRACT

The Global Learning Wiki activity connects students around the world on a wiki website. In this activity, students post questions about issues of interest to them and then respond to one another's questions, thus learning from students in other countries on the wiki website. In this activity students not only learn technology skills but also gain a global awareness as it pertains to K–12 schooling. This activity is beneficial to students in terms of gaining experience in partnership, collaboration, global awareness, international perspective, and much more.

BACKGROUND AND PURPOSE

A fast-changing world in an era of globalization has influenced education and redefined the skills that students need for success in the twenty-first century. The Partnership for 21st Century Skills (2008), a national organization, indicated core subjects and twenty-first century themes, life and career skills, learning and innovation skills, and information, media, and technology skills (p. 13) as the main skill domains required of today's students. In the realm of twenty-first century themes, it includes global awareness and a variety of literacies in economy, civics, health, and environment.

Teachers have been generally successful in helping students master core subjects; however, as the world and the workforce become increasingly connected internationally, educating students to be globally competent becomes a priority. The Asia Society (Mansilla & Jackson, 2011) indicated four capacities that globally competent students should possess: (a) investigating the world beyond their immediate environment; (b) recognizing perspectives, others' and their own; (c) communicating ideas effectively with diverse audiences; and (d) taking action to improve conditions (p. 11). To help students develop these capacities, teacher educators should act accordingly.

One of the goals of today's teacher education programs is to prepare preservice teachers to be globally competent. Although studying abroad is an effective way to learn values, languages, and cultures of other countries, very few college students actually have the opportunity to do so. The Institute of International Education (2012) reported that the number of students studying abroad for a single academic year represents only one percent of the total enrollment in U.S. higher education.

With this activity, students work beyond traditional ways of acquiring information by making direct contact with educators and students in other nations. Using technology, preservice teachers build connections with educators and students around the world to gain firsthand knowledge and valuable experience.

LEARNING OBJECTIVES

After completing the activity, students should be able to:

- use technology efficiently to share and exchange information and knowledge with educators and students in other nations;
- demonstrate knowledge of other cultures and their education practices;
- adapt their behavior to interact effectively with those who are culturally different; and
- build global partnerships with educators and students in other nations.

PROCEDURE

The instructor must prearrange with an overseas educator and his or her class to participate in the project. Such contacts can be made through personal or peer relationships or through some already existing Internet sites whose purpose is to link classrooms around the world (see the last paragraph of this chapter for suggestions).

Phase 1: What We Already Know and What We Want to Know

Form groups of students and have each group discuss or research some topics about the country that they will be contacting. The instructor can choose topics based on the curriculum objectives of his or her class. Have students first share with their group members what they already know about the country, based on the topic discussed. Then students list questions that they would like to ask the overseas class. These questions will be posted on a wiki website that the students create in Phase 2.

Phase 2: Build a Wiki Website and Begin Conversations

1. Create a wiki website at wikispaces.com.

   - The wiki website is used as a space for sharing information, ideas, thoughts, images, videos, audios, documents, and so forth, by the overseas class and your class.
   - The wiki is created by one of the class members. Then he or she adds all of the other class members as members of the wiki so that everyone can contribute to or modify the wiki. The class instructor can also do this step.

2. Develop the home page of the wiki website with pictures, audios/ videos, and an introductory statement.

   - The home page includes a photo of the class and an introductory statement that is well structured, well written, and engaging.
   - The class photo and all other pictures are of good quality and of appropriate size.
   - A short greeting video or audio includes at least one sentence that you speak in your partner's language.

3. List questions, each one on an individual page of the wiki, covering topics that you are interested in learning about from the overseas class. The goal of the Questions and Responses is to share perspectives on the questions raised by both groups.

4. E-mail the address of your wiki website to the overseas educator, and invite his and her class to participate in the wiki.

Please note that the overseas educator and his or her students will request to join the wiki website once they have received the address of the wiki. Have one of the class members monitor the requests from the overseas class. The students or the instructor can also create bulk usernames and passwords and send them to the overseas class so that they can access the wiki site easily.

Phase 3: Create Responses to the Questions

1. Discuss with the group members how to respond to the questions raised by the overseas class.

2. Besides the written text, suggest that students' responses include pictures, hyperlinks, videos, audios, or other types of media to enhance the information presented.

3. Work on the responses to the questions.

- Please note that English might be the second language of members in the overseas class; therefore, if voice is used, students must speak clearly at a slower pace and add captions/text or provide transcripts to all the multimedia materials they create.
- To ensure that the overseas educator can easily access and open the documents created by your class, post all multimedia materials onto the wiki and convert documents to PDF format.

Phase 4: Presentation

The purpose of the presentation is to share with the whole class what you did and what you learned. The presentation should be well structured and proceed systematically. The instructor can also arrange a joint presentation with the overseas class via Skype or other videoconferencing technology if the presentation time works for both classes. Requirements for the presentation are as follows:

1. The students can use PowerPoint, Prezi, Poster, or just the wiki site for the presentation.
2. Students gather information about the overseas partner and his or her class:

   - The country and school (use Google Earth or a map to identify)
   - Official language, education system and structure, and so forth
   - Photos of the overseas partner, his or her students, school, classroom, school environment, and so forth
   - School or class information
   - Technology facility in the school and classroom and how they use it

3. Report responses to the questions and present the materials received from the overseas class that you created.

   - Report the similarities and differences on the questions/topics discussed.
   - Report anything that surprised you as well as your overall thoughts.
   - Show at least one video. The video could be something that you received from the partner class, popular songs from the partner country that you searched from the Internet, and so forth.

After the presentation, write a thank-you e-mail to the partner class as a completion of the project and to show gratitude for their participation.

Grading Rubric

Students will be graded on their contributions and efforts on the activity, organization of the wiki website, quality of the responses, use of technology, and presentation.

ADDITIONAL COMMENTS

Prearranging with an overseas educator and his or her class is a key for the success of the activity. The author's connection to an overseas school came from the help of the Office for International and Intercultural Education at her university. If you do not have ready access to an overseas school, consult with the international office at your university for potential connections. Other helpful resources for finding and connecting international educators are through global social networks, such as ePals (http://www.epals.com/), iEARN (www.iearn.org), Global Nomads (www.gng.org), or Skype in the classroom (https://education.skype.com/)

	Proficient	Acceptable	Unacceptable
Collaboration/effort	Student contributes equally with other class/group members in the wiki site building, contacting overseas partner, researching, writing, and editing.	Student provides minimal assistance to the class/group members in the wiki site tasks.	Student provides no assistance to the class/group members in any of the wiki site tasks.
Wiki site	Content is well organized and formatted throughout the wiki.	Content is logically organized and formatted for the most part.	Clear or logical organizational structure is lacking, or the formatting is cluttered and inconsistent throughout the wiki.
Questions and responses	Shows evidence of thorough preparation with substantial information.	Shows moderate amount of evidence of preparation with somewhat sufficient information.	Shows little or no evidence of preparation with insufficient information.
Use of technology	Beside written text, responses demonstrate strong use of technology with at least 3 different formats to enhance the information presented.	Beside written text, responses somewhat demonstrate acceptable use of technology with one or two different formats.	Responses are written text only.
Presentation	A mostly seamless presentation. Students present information in logical sequence. Things go smoothly and any issues result from unavoidable factors.	A few simple mistakes that could have been avoided with more adequate preparation. Information could be presented in a more logical sequence.	Student frequently appears unorganized. There is no sequence of information.

Table 6.1.

REFERENCES

Mansilla, V. B., & Jackson, T. (2011). *Educating for Global Competence: Preparing Our Youth to Engage the World*. New York: Asia Society.

The Partnership for 21st Century Skills. (2008). 21st century skills, education, and competitiveness. Retrieved from http://www.p21.org/storage/documents/ 21st_century_skills_education_and_competitiveness_guide.pdf.

U.S. Department of Education. (2012, May 3). Broadening the spirit of respect and cooperation for the global public good. Retrieved from http://www.ed.gov/news/speeches/broadening-spirit-respect-and-cooperation-global-public-good.

Activity 7

The Arrow Always Points to the Self: Preservice Teacher Learning Through Blurred Geopolitical Identities

Jubin Rahatzad, Hannah Sasser, JoAnn Phillion, and Suniti Sharma

The fact is, we are mixed in with one another in ways that most national systems of education have not dreamed of.
—Edward W. Said, 1993

ABSTRACT

This activity engages preservice teachers in introspection and reflection around social constructions of the self and other. The goal is to enhance intercultural competence through recognition of differences within intercultural interaction. The activity juxtaposes the cultural practices of the "Nacirema" tribe, described in the article "Body Rituals among the Nacirema" (Miner, 1956), with contemporary practices of Iranians, in their plurality, as a means of troubling normalized conceptions of the self and other. Suggestions are made for strategic implementation of the activity for white monoculture preservice teachers for the purpose of raising social justice awareness.

BACKGROUND AND PURPOSE

The following activity is used in a foundational teacher education course based on social justice oriented multiculturalism. The purpose of the course is to raise social awareness through an examination of multiple topics that play a role in educational experiences and opportunities for students. While the course is primarily focused on a U.S. context, where most preservice teachers in the teacher education program envision their futures, the course pushes forward an international mindset that encourages intercultural competence.

Furthermore, equity is a theme threaded throughout the curriculum of the course in order to allow preservice teachers to inquire about equitable student opportunities and teaching practices. The activity described is one of many that turns the mirror onto the preservice teacher (self) in order to understand how the student (other) is socially constructed. Therefore, otherness and equity are key themes throughout the course with the purpose of cultivating intercultural competence among preservice teachers.

The proposed activity starts with ethnocentric preservice teachers (Cushner, 2012) and assists in the decentering (Buendía, 2000) of the self's normalized sense of being through the familiarization of the other.

This activity is designed to challenge preservice teachers' geopolitical preconceptions about the self and other. The vast majority of students typically enrolled in the class are white, self-described "middle-class" females from monocultural backgrounds. To aid in the decentering of U.S./American identity and culture, students read Miner's (1956) "Body Rituals among the Nacirema" prior to class discussion.

On average, only 10 percent of students are familiar with the article, and therefore, when it is revealed that "Nacirema" is "American" spelled backwards and that the author is viewing Americans from an "outsider's" perspective, most students experience something akin to an "ah-ha!" moment. This framework is used as a point of departure to discuss how a contemporary group, Iran/Iranians, is othered within U.S. culture and imagination.

Exploration of how groups of people are abnormalized or othered through cultural discourse is an important component in the preparation of teachers for diverse classroom settings (Grant & Zwier, 2011). The geopolitical component of discussion between decentering American identity and culture (from the 1950s) and familiarizing contemporary Iranian lifestyles is beneficial for preservice teachers to engage with macro-level theorizations about various groups of people represented within U.S. classrooms.

Engagement with the other and awareness of the self are part of the process of developing a political consciousness (Freire, 2000) that relates to preservice teachers' academic expectations of future students as influenced by perceived/known backgrounds (Milner, 2010). Explicit discussions about preservice teachers' preconceptions of those who are different from them foster greater cultural awareness and impact learning based on relationships within the classroom (Cushner, McClelland, & Safford, 2012).

Relationships between teachers and students is of utmost importance as illustrated by the demographic imperative that highlights the cultural disparity between the more than 40 percent of U.S. public school students from ethnic/racial minority groups (a number that is continually growing) and the 90 percent of U.S. teachers who come from white monoculture backgrounds (a number that is relatively static) (Zeichner, 2009). Engaging with perceived and/or real differences between constructions of the self and other can influence future teaching practice.

LEARNING OBJECTIVES

The learning objectives of the described activity include the following:

- understanding of how the self is socially constructed;
- understanding of how the social construction of the other is based on the self;
- introspection and reflection around negotiations of difference through power;
- development of intercultural competence and awareness to foster understanding of the role that preconceptions play in teaching practice and impact students' educational opportunities;
- exposure to discussion of teaching practices that contest the muting of difference within the classroom, such as colorblindness; and
- engagement with challenging and sensitive issues in education.

PROCEDURE

As part of the readings on American identity, students are assigned Horace Miner's 1956 article "Body Rituals among the Nacirema." With an anthropological perspective, Miner detailed the customs and rituals of what he called the "undescribed tribe" (p. 503) of the Nacirema. Many students are surprised and sometimes shocked not just to read about the seemingly strange customs and rituals of this tribe, but also by the fact that they had been previously unaware of the tribe's existence since they inhabit land in North America between Canada and Mexico.

Some salient characteristics of the Nacirema tribe members are their fixation on their physical appearance and their obsession with youthfulness. Miner explained,

> The fundamental belief underlying the whole system appears to be that the human body is ugly and that its natural tendency is to debility and disease. Incarcerated in such a body, man's only hope is to avert these characteristics through the use of the powerful influences of ritual and ceremony. (p. 503)

These rituals include "inserting a small bundle of hog hairs into the mouth, along with certain magical powders, and then moving the bundle in a highly formalized series of gestures" (p. 504), an activity that describes tooth brushing.

Another Nacirema ritual is the initiation of children into the "private and secret" "mysteries" (p. 503) that are carried out in the household shrines and that are not spoken of prior to this coming of age. This represents toilet training and bodily hygiene. Last, men in the Nacirema tribe engage in a ritual that entails "scraping and lacerating the surface of the face with a sharp instrument" (shaving with a razor) and women "bake their heads in small ovens for about an hour" (beauty salon hairdryers) (p. 505).

Most students agree with Miner's assessment that "most of the population shows definite masochistic tendencies" (p. 505), as illustrated by their seemingly painful customs. Students are instructed to anonymously write their impressions of the Nacirema and their practices (note: prior to any discussion of the article, students who are familiar with the Nacirema are asked to not reveal what they know).

Written responses are collected by the instructor and redistributed to students so that each student shares a classmate's response aloud. Reactions to Nacirema society include details regarding the absurdity of practices like those listed above and often express shock and dismay at the cruelness of the described society. A few responses convey outrage at the barbarity of certain practices, while other responses temper the expressed opinion with acceptance through some degree of cultural relativity.

One of the authors of this chapter (Jubin Rahatzad) preferred to reveal Miner's intentions by asking that a student with previous familiarity of the Nacirema explain it to the class. Of the twelve times that Jubin has taught using this activity, in only one class did a student not previously familiar with the article realize that Miner was describing American society prior to intentional disclosure.

After students express amazement and/or surprise at Miner's inversion of normality, the instructor provides a brief description of the context in which Miner was working and why he chose to test his fellow academics in order to demonstrate how an outsider anthropologist may "other" U.S. society and culture and how U.S. or Eurocentric scholars routinely "other" differences in societies outside their own.

Further discussion ensues as students consider for the first time what the practices and customs that seem familiar to them might look like from another's viewpoint. They go back through the article, examining it from a new perspective. They realize, for example, that the "imposing temple" (p. 505) of the tribe's medicine men is a description of a hospital and that the "vestal maidens who move sedately about the temple chambers in distinctive costume and headdress" (p. 505) are nurses.

As class discussion centers around the construction of normality/abnormality of societies and cultures, some students make comparisons to contemporary U.S. society and some students refer to the three additional assigned readings (Durning, 2002; Randolph, 2008; Shah, 2004). From this point, the focus of the class is shifted toward a contemporary constructed other, Iran. Jubin describes his experience teaching this part of the activity as a U.S.-born Iranian.

For the second part of this activity, Jubin writes the word "Iran" on the board and instructs students to anonymously write down what comes to mind when they think of Iran. In only two of the twelve courses in which Jubin has used this activity have students surmised his identity as a U.S.-born Iranian.

Jubin often leaves ambiguous many aspects of his identity, both visible and invisible. Based on Jubin's life experience, people have often assumed him to be of Latino descent (particularly Puerto Rican), and students rarely inquire about his background on their own. Jubin always urges students, whether they know of his Iranian background or not, to set aside political correctness and concerns about rudeness when they write down their thoughts about Iran. Written responses are collected and redistributed, and each student shares a classmate's thoughts aloud.

Student responses usually include references and descriptions such as: nuclear weapons, camels, dirty, dark, not modern, no women's rights, Aladdin, desert, poor, Islam, 9/11, terrorism, oil, and sand. As with the Nacirema, some of the written comments reveal absolute distaste, while other comments justify the othered identity through cultural relativism. The majority of descriptions demonstrate either a lack of knowledge about Iran or a knowledge based on U.S. war-mongering media representations.

Jubin refrains from providing a historical background that would demonstrate the complete turnaround in pre- and post-1979 (Islamic Revolution in Iran) political relations between Iran and the United States. Instead, Jubin focuses on contemporary Iran through a slideshow conversation and foregrounds what is invisible about Iran within contemporary U.S. society, especially in the aftermath of the "war on terror" since 2001.

This multicultural education course experiences a high amount of student resistance throughout all sections, and there are likely students who discredit Jubin's representations of Iran as biased and who may therefore resist thinking about how people and groups are othered. This is one possible downfall to engaging with a highly vilified group; however, the intention is to show how the familiar can be made unfamiliar and the unfamiliar can be made familiar. In other words, how do the self and the other relate to one another through difference?

The intention is to demonstrate falsities that construct difference, but also to engage perceived and/or real differences. The slideshow is made up of a variety of images such as Iranians picnicking in a park, female equestrian archers, youths engaged in "water gun fights," green and mountainous landscapes (unlike the stereotyped deserts of the Arabian peninsula), cities (Tehran's population is conservatively over 12 million people), women with elaborate hairstyles being shown off by almost nonexistent head cover on the streets of Tehran, women of various ethnicities (e.g., Kurd, Lor, Gilaki) in rural settings wearing colorful "chadors," and Christian and Jewish communities.

Most of the images bring forth candid reactions from the preservice teachers. The utilization of preservice teachers' candid reactions to the various images of life in Iran enables a discussion about the unknown aspects of the other. While the discussion differs for each class, the main point of the activity is to avoid uncritically accepting a given discourse about those different from oneself.

Islam is often a focus of discussion since Iran is majority Muslim, and this topic includes the conflation of Arab and Muslim identity (as monolithically homogenized in the U.S. popular imaginary), which is deconstructed through explanation of Iranian/Persian identity and other Middle Eastern identities (within and across ethnic, national, and religious identities—for example, Christian Armenian-Iranians, Turkish Kurd/Kurdish Turk, Syrian Arab Jew, diversity within Islam beyond simplistic Sunni/Shia conceptions, and diversity within Orthodox Christianity).

Some students begin to grapple with and/or understand how assumptions and stereotypes they have constructed about Iranian society and culture have been informed by the popular news and media that simplistically portray Iran as a culturally backwards hotbed of terrorist activity. Connections are made back to Miner's (1956) Nacirema example to illustrate how the familiar can be made unfamiliar through techniques of othering used on groups deemed as inferior. Class discussion can explicitly or implicitly engage knowledge production and how knowledges are used to construct understandings of the world (Mignolo, 2012).

As a closing activity, students are instructed to reflect on implications for education and teaching through writing. Time is given for writing and sharing. Debriefing occurs in three stages: after the Nacirema, after Iran, and after reflecting on how the concepts of self and other construct differences and expectations for educational settings. Some student reflections move beyond "I will not judge my students without getting to know them" and acknowledge that societal bias is inherent in our ways of being. This activity is part of a semester-long process of engaging with difference and recognizing power differentials in society.

ADDITIONAL COMMENTS

Iran is a useful example for engaging the extremes of othering from a U.S. perspective. Instructors not familiar with Iran can use the article "Are Americans Ready for Democracy?" (Berreby, 2011) that uses Miner's (1956) strategy to discuss the United States from an "Iranian" or outsider perspective through hypothetical news/editorial rhetoric. This can counterbalance preservice teachers' ideas about Iran. However, there are other contexts than Iran that may serve as useful alternatives for instructors who are not familiar with Iran.

For example, "Islamophobia" can be employed to juxtapose Miner's article with the film *Reel Bad Arabs: How Hollywood Vilifies a People* (Earp & Jhally, 2006). Another example may be to trouble the positive stereotype of Asian-Americans, which is based on the homogenization and "essentialization" of all Asians into a monolithic group. There are also many other examples of groups that have been othered within/outside the dominant Eurocentric U.S. perspective.

The decision to use Iran as an example was based on the fact that African-American/black identities and Latino identities are often overrepresented in multicultural education class readings and activities. There are benefits to this activity in the attempt to break up the black/white binary or the immigrant = Latino essentialization. The activity directly addresses the conflation of Arab and Muslim identity and broadens the discussion of Middle Eastern identity during the reactionary "war on terror" policy and ideology.

One of the authors of this chapter (Hannah Sasser) teaches a foundational course for preservice teachers to explore the teaching profession, which is taught in conjunction with the multicultural education course that uses this activity. Hannah has observed that many preservice teachers have reached adulthood and entered college without giving serious thought to the construction of their own identity, particularly in relation to the other. In their writings and in class discussions, many students use the word "normal" to describe their backgrounds, upbringings, and educational experiences.

This view of the self seems indicative of the idea that any deviations from their "normal" (white, Christian, middle-class) way of being is abnormal and, quite possibly, wrong. Teacher education can challenge such ethnocentric thinking by placing focus on preservice teachers' engagements with cultural others through activities like the one presented. Introspection and reflection on the self develops intercultural competence and awareness when placed at the core of teacher education.

The increasing diversity within U.S. K–12 classrooms demands culturally attentive teachers. Teachers who are aware of issues that impact equitable and equal educational opportunities are more effective in working with students to reconceptualize the social world. The ability to work with students of different backgrounds—others—requires adaptive intercultural skill because there is no prepackaged plan for engaging in the educational experience with students who embody different backgrounds and lives.

Such considerations are crucial for the aim of social justice and equity within education. Ultimately, as teachers understand themselves through socially constructed identities and realities, the potential to become familiar with others can benefit classroom practice. Teacher educators have an ethical responsibility to instigate exploration of how otherness impacts educational equity.

REFERENCES

Berreby, D. (2011, February 22). Are Americans ready for democracy? Retrieved from http://bigthink.com/Mind-Matters/are-americans-ready-for-democracy.

Buendía, E. (2000). Power and possibility: The construction of a pedagogical practice. *Teaching and Teacher Education, 16*(2), 147–63.

Cushner, K. (2012). Planting seeds for peace: Are they growing in the right direction? *International Journal of Intercultural Relations, 36*(2), 161–68.

Cushner, K., McClelland, A., & Safford, P. (2012). *Human Diversity in Education: An Intercultural Approach* (7th ed.). Boston: McGraw-Hill.

Durning, A. T. (2002). Just a cup of coffee? In B. Bigelow & B. Peterson (Eds.), *Rethinking globalization: Teaching for justice in an unjust world* (pp. 243–44). Milwaukee, WI: Rethinking Schools Press.

Earp, J., & Jhally, S. (Directors). (2006). *Reel Bad Arabs: How Hollywood Vilifies a People* [Motion picture]. United States: Media Education Foundation.

Freire, P. (2000). *Pedagogy of the Oppressed*. (M. B. Ramos, Trans., 30th ann. ed.). New York: Continuum. (Original work published 1970).

Grant, C. A., & Zwier, E. (2011). Intersectionality and student outcomes: Sharpening the struggle against racism, sexism, classism, ableism, heterosexism, nationalism, and linguistic, religious, and geographical discrimination in teaching and learning. *Multicultural Perspectives, 13*(4), 181–88.

Mignolo, W. D. (2012). *Local Histories/Global Designs: Coloniality, Subaltern Knowledges, and Border Thinking*. Princeton: Princeton University Press.

Milner, H. R., IV. (2010). *Start Where You Are, But Don't Stay There: Understanding Diversity, Opportunity Gaps, and Teaching in Today's Classrooms*. Cambridge, MA: Harvard Education Press.

Miner, H. (1956). Body ritual among the Nacirema. *American Anthropologist, 58*(3), 503–7.

Randolph, B. (2008). I didn't know there were cities in Africa! *Teaching Tolerance, 43*(34), 36–43.

Said, E. W. (1993). *Culture and Imperialism*. New York: Vintage.

Shah, S. (2004). The tiniest trash bin. *Orion Magazine, 23*(6), 80.

Zeichner, K. M. (2009). *Teacher Education and the Struggle for Social Justice*. New York: Routledge.

Activity 8

The Coalition for Creative Projects

Schea N. Fissel

ABSTRACT

University-based organizations and institutes provide a collaborative medium toward enacting change that is personally meaningful, societally important, and has the ability to sustain impact. By using a methodological approach to empowerment ingrained in a collaborative learning and action structure, students are provided the opportunity to develop a personally meaningful connection to important cultural/societal issues by learning a process for enacting change in local groups, organizations, or societies. This approach will not only promote the ideals of equality and justice in society, but will also collaboratively seek change for the greater good.

BACKGROUND AND PURPOSE

Empowerment, the act of obtaining power or empowering others, is frequently discussed in the social justice literature as a catalyst for societal change (Cattaneo & Chapman, 2010). Cattaneo and Chapman discussed empowerment in the context of social media suggesting that the acquisition of power results in an observable impact in social contexts. They further defined methods toward achieving empowerment, including six principal methods in their model: setting personally meaningful power-oriented goals (wanting to make changes), self-efficacy (believing one can make changes), knowledge (how to make changes), competence (the tools to make changes), action (actually making changes), and impact (the effects of the changes made).

The concept of a university-based group aimed at empowering students to make sustainable changes in society and promote cultural competence can be implemented effectively on a smaller scale within the structure of the classroom or through classroom projects. Implementing collaborative activities or learning groups within the classroom promotes the components proposed in Cattaneo and Chapman's (2010) model of empowerment. The most important components in application of this model are: (a) that there is a clear method for how to achieve impact on society, and (b) that the students are allowed to create ideas for change that hold a good deal of personal incentive or meaning.

Adams, Bell, and Griffin (2007) defined social justice as "both a process and a goal" (p. 1) suggesting its goal should be parity in both power and participation across societal groups and its process should be innovative and highly collaborative. Our modern, global society is evolving to parallel this ideal of equality by collaboration. This evolution is most apparent in the process of weaving theory, concepts, and methods of global citizenship, cultural competence, and social justice into the academic fabric of higher education's curriculum.

For example, Case Western Reserve University, following in the footsteps of alumni including Louis Stokes and Stephanie Tubbs Jones, has pioneered the Social Justice Institute. This Institute employs the concepts of equality by collaboration in creating a group that seeks to advance "education, research and community engagement that inspire creative, sustainable, and most importantly just solutions to societal problems" (Case Western Reserve University, n.d., p. 1). Other universities have developed their own organizations dedicated to social justice (e.g., University of Michigan [MCHANGE] and Western Michigan University [Haenicke Institute]).

LEARNING OUTCOMES

A creative project and interdisciplinary collaborative group structure, such as the Coalition for Change described below, can be integrated into a classroom project. As a result of implementing this project, students will:

- create a social entrepreneurship plan (SEP) with the ultimate goal of achieving impact on a local group, organization, or society;
- demonstrate principles of collaboration and effective communication with peers in developing a SEP;
- identify goals of their project, rationale, resources, and methods required to enact proposed change, potential partnerships/collaborations, and the anticipated impact on the targeted group organization or society;
- engage in discussion about barriers of implementing a SEP in an applicable group, organization, or society and will problem solve for possible solutions; and

- present their SEP and discuss anticipated results, potential parameters of impact, and barriers after implementation of the SEP.

PROCESS

Students will be divided into small groups of at least two participants. Groups may vary based on student interest/incentive. Small groups should first identify a maladaptive process/method/construct within an applicable group, organization, or society that they wish to change. Pictures of both micro- and macro-social issues may be presented to initiate topic selection. A list of questions to facilitate topic selection is found in Appendix A at the end of this chapter.

Within their small groups, once a process/method/construct is selected, students will identify the following parameters: description of group/organization/society and context, statement of the process/method/construct to change, summary of intended change, specific method/plan for change, specific goals and objectives of intended change, rationale/support for change, statement of anticipated benefit, statement of anticipated impact, identification of multidisciplinary/interdisciplinary collaborations or community partnerships, and any resources/funding/budgetary considerations for enacting the SEP.

Ideally, the Coalition for Change would extend across the entire semester to allow for actualizing implementation of the SEP. Running this project across a semester allows for increased comprehension of methods/process and collaborative problem solving to enact change, and an opportunity to implement the SEP and observe the impact following implementation of the SEP. However, this project may be implemented on a smaller scale within a single class to provide students with an introduction to collaborative interdisciplinary teamwork, critical thinking skills, and social problem solving.

Processes for implementing the Coalition for Change across a semester and within a single class are provided. In both modifications of this project, students should be encouraged to creatively design and select personally meaningful plans to address disparities in groups, organizations, or societies that the student has membership in or is motivated by. Instructions for implementing the Coalition for Change are as follows:

Single Class Implementation

A: Group Discussion and Formation

1. Students will be presented with a variety of pictures depicting both micro-societal issues (e.g., communication partner/peer training to promote increased and inclusive social interactions in students with disabilities) and macro-societal issues (e.g., inclusionary classroom practices for students with disabilities).
2. As a class, students will discuss interests/preferences regarding groups, organizations, or societies they are interested in changing. Constructs for facilitating group discussion and topic selection are indicated in Appendix A.
3. Students will form small groups based on interests, passions, and motivation. Again, students should form groups with at least two members.
4. Within small groups, students should be allotted time to develop a hypothetical social entrepreneurship plan (SEP) including description of the targeted group/organization/society and context, statement of the process/method/construct to change, summary of intended change, specific method/plan for change, specific goals and objectives of intended change, rationale/support for change, statement of anticipated benefit, statement of anticipated impact, identification of multidisciplinary/interdisciplinary collaborations or community partnerships, and any resources/funding/budgetary considerations for enacting the SEP.
5. The final SEP product may be developed in any medium including PowerPoint, written report, pictorial depiction, dramatic interpretation, and so forth—it is the choice of each individual group.
6. Students will present their hypothetical SEP in the desired medium.
7. Time for discussion of each group's SEP should be allotted. Discussion may include questions, feedback, problem solving, or modifications to the SEP.

Semester Implementation

A: Group Discussion and Formation

1. Students will be presented with a variety of pictures depicting both micro societal issues (e.g., communication partner/peer training to promote increased and inclusive social interactions in students with disabilities) and macro societal issues (e.g., inclusionary classroom practices for students with disabilities).

2. As a class, students will discuss interests/preferences regarding groups, organizations, or societies they are interested in changing. Constructs for facilitating group discussion and topic selection are indicated in Appendix A.
3. Students will prepare and discuss any experiences where they have or sought to change an established system or idea.
4. Students will form groups based on interests, passions, and motivation. Again, students should form groups with at least two members.
5. Students should establish roles within groups and set expectations for communication and collaboration. Students will dictate roles and expectations and submit this document for professor/teacher review.

B: Development of the Social Entrepreneurship Plan (SEP)

1. Students will progressively create a group SEP. The SEP will include the following primary sections: description of targeted group/organization/society and context, statement of the process/method/construct to change, summary of intended change, specific method/plan for change, specific goals and objectives of intended change, rationale/support for change, statement of anticipated benefit, statement of anticipated impact, identification of multidisciplinary/interdisciplinary collaborations or community partnerships, and any resources/funding/budgetary considerations for enacting the SEP.
2. An evaluation matrix is provided in Appendix B for measurement.
3. Students should be allotted time within class to engage in both group discussions about development of each section and written development of each section.
4. Students should submit their SEP to a partner group for revision/editing and most importantly, suggestions. Partner groups will return the edited document to its owners who will make secondary revisions/edits based on the evaluation matrix provided in Appendix B.
5. Students will submit their SEP to the instructor for review. Instructors provide revisions, edits, and suggestions based on the evaluation matrix (Appendix B).
6. The document will be returned to students with "enough" available semester time for implementation.

C: Implementation and impact

1. Students will implement or take the foundational steps in their SEP.
2. Students will observe and informally record impact, repercussions, adversities, and/or successes in implementing their SEP.

D: Final group discussion

1. Groups will present all sections of their SEP to the collective class in any form of medium applicable to the content of their project.
2. After presenting the methods of their SEP to the class, groups will discuss their impressions of impact, repercussions, adversities, and/or successes.
3. Time should be allotted or integrated into each presentation for questions and group discussion.

APPENDIX A

Constructs to Facilitate SEP Development

1. Have students anonymously list extracurricular activities, leisure-based activities, social and vocational groups they participate in, organizations they are a part of, cultural affiliations, religious affiliations, socioeconomic status, and experiences they have had with societal and disenfranchised groups.
2. The teacher may collect the students' lists and redistribute these throughout the class. Students may present the list provided to them.
3. Pass out the following list of questions for group discussion:

    a) What are the mission/goals of the group, organization, society, or culture?
    b) What are the established systems or processes in the identified group, organization, society, or culture?
    c) What do you like about these established systems/processes? How do these systems/processes improve group functioning or further the mission/goals of the group?
    d) What concepts are these established systems/processes grounded in? What function do they serve? Are they evidence based? Do they accomplish the mission/goals of the group, organization, culture, or society?
    e) What are some maladaptive systems/processes of the group, organization, society, or culture?
    f) What concepts are these established systems/processes grounded in? What function do they serve? Are they evidence based? Do they accomplish the goals/mission of the group, organization, society, or culture?
    g) How do these maladaptive systems/processes impede the progress of the group, organization, society, or culture? Do these maladaptive systems/processes benefit anyone in the group, organization, society, or culture?

h) Are there systems/processes you feel could be implemented or modified to accomplish the goals/mission of the group, organization, society, or culture? Are your ideas achievable?

i) What level of impact would you hope to achieve by implementing or modifying new systems/processes?

4. Allow time for other students to provide feedback and/or ask questions.

APPENDIX B

Parameter	Description	Word Count Limit	Evaluation
Title and Contact Information	Brief title and demographic information of those involved	N/A	5 points
Description of Group/Organization/Society and Context	Should briefly describe applicable group/systems, influences and motivations.	300 words or less	10 points
Statement of the Process/Method/Construct to Change	Should briefly describe systems of the group which result in maladaptive practices	150 words or less	10 points
Summary of Intended Change	Brief, succinct overview of proposed plan for change	50 words or less	10 points
Methods/Plan	Step by step detailed outline for enacting all components of Plan	N/A	10 points
Specific Goals and Objectives of Plan/Project	3–5 long term goals with specific short term objectives	N/A	10 points
Rationale/Support and Statement of Proposed Benefit	Review of applicable current practices and evidenced based practices. Students should summarize at least 5 peer-reviewed professional publications to support plan	300 words or less	10 points
Anticipated Impact	Identification of cohort(s) systems	100 words or less	10 points
Collaboration/Partnerships	Identification of multidisciplinary/interdisciplinary collaborations or community partnerships	N/A	10 points
Budget/Resources/Funding	Detailed description of funding allocation, as well as intended sources of funding	N/A	10 points
References	APA citation of at least 5 peer reviewed professional publications	N/A	5 points

Total Available Points: 100

Table 8.1.

REFERENCES

Adams, M., Bell, L. A., & Griffin, P. (2007). *Teaching for diversity and social justice*. New York: Routledge.

Case Western Reserve University. (n.d.). Case Western Reserve University Social Justice Institute. Social Justice at Case Western Reserve University. Retrieved from http://case.edu/socialjustice/index.html.

Cattaneo, L. B., & Chapman, A. R. (2010). The process of empowerment. A model for use in research and practice. *American Psychologist, 65*(7), 646–59.

REFERENCES CONSULTED

Caldwell, K., Harris, S. P., & Renko, M. (2012). The potential of social entrepreneurship: Conceptual tools for applying citizenship theory to policy and practice. *Intellectual and Developmental Disabilities, 50*(6), 505–18.

Payne, K. T. (2011). Ethics of disability: Foundation of the profession of speech-language pathology. *Seminars in Speech and Language, 32*, 279–88.

Activity 9

Conversation Partner Experience: A Win-Win Culture Learning Encounter

Kenneth Cushner

ABSTRACT

The university offers significant opportunities for meaningful intercultural interaction between domestic and international students, thus allowing teacher-education students to learn about others' cultures, as well as their challenges entering a new culture and educational system. Application to the new immigrant or English Language Learner (ELL) experience in U.S. schools is considered.

BACKGROUND AND PURPOSE

U.S. teacher-education students typically enter the profession holding stereotypic perceptions of those different from themselves that are heavily shaped by media and overly simplistic images portrayed in popular culture and the Internet. Few have had direct meaningful firsthand experiences interacting with people from other cultural backgrounds—especially with those from overseas.

This is somewhat surprising given that universities are among the most diverse organizations in the world, with an increasing number of students coming from abroad joining those who represent the increasing diversity of the nation. The university with its significant opportunities for meaningful intercultural interaction provides an exceptional learning laboratory to achieve these goals, especially for teacher-education students who are certain to face increasingly culturally diverse classrooms and communities.

The unfortunate truth, however, is that the desired intercultural interactions rarely occur with the depth and successful outcomes that are assumed. In Australia, studies have found that domestic students were not as interested in intercultural contact as were their international student counterparts (Nesdale & Todd, 1993). In New Zealand, Ward and her colleagues (2005) reported that although domestic students tended to have positive perceptions of international students, their subsequent interactions and intercultural friendships were rare.

In studies in England, Ireland, and South Africa, domestic students report a number of communication and language challenges, as well as the possibility of making cultural faux pas, that led to an avoidance of the other (Peacock & Harrison, 2009; Dunne, 2009; Le Roux, 2010; Hyde & Ruth, 2002). Sanchez (2004) reported similar results in Spain, with barriers to interaction deriving from language and cultural differences. Finally, Groeppel-Klein, Germelmann, and Glaum (2010) reported that even in a border university that had a specific intercultural mission and priority serving students in Germany and Poland, significant intercultural interaction did not occur over time.

The situation appears similar in the United States where domestic students report positive, yet stereotypical views about international students, and perceive a range of threats and anxieties (Spencer-Rodgers, 2001). Halualani, Chitgopekar, Morrison, and Dodge (2004) found that, while students even on multicultural university campuses that promote diversity report interacting with international students, these interactions tend to be perceived as less important, separate from their personal friendship networks, or occur in brief one-time exchanges. Many assume that because they are surrounded by diversity, it automatically translates into substantial encounters.

The literature across the board suggests that even when institutions stress the importance of intercultural interaction, among domestically diverse students as well as between domestic and international students, these interactions are limited, often fleeting, and generate a source of anxiety for students, teachers, and administrators alike. This should be of grave concern, especially given the increased emphasis to enhance intercultural competence that is encouraged by most university administrators and required in the global workforce.

LEARNING OBJECTIVES

Developing intercultural sensitivity does not happen through cognitive inputs alone—direct, impactful, reflective experience is an essential element (Cushner, 2007). As a result of this activity, international students:

- practice spoken English, and
- learn about U.S. culture firsthand.

Domestic students:

- learn about another culture firsthand,
- gain an understanding of the cultural adjustment challenges international students (and perhaps their families) face,
- develop friendships with non-U.S. students (many for the first time), and
- consider how what they have experienced and learned applies to students and families they are certain to encounter in schools.

PROCESS

Meaningful interaction tends not to happen on its own simply because people are in the vicinity of one another. Classroom instructors can be instrumental in encouraging and supporting structured opportunities for meaningful intercultural engagement. Many international students on campus desire to practice spoken English and to interact outside of the classroom with domestic students. Many international offices arrange such encounters.

1. Pair an international student and a domestic student as Conversation Partners.
2. Students are expected to meet with their partner for at least one hour a week, each with a task at hand. They should reflect upon their weekly experiences in a journal.
3. International students are provided an opportunity to practice oral communication and become more familiar with a domestic student.
4. Domestic teacher-education students are asked to learn about their partner's culture as well their adjustment to life in the United States.
5. Halfway through the experience, domestic students can reflect upon (through writing or discussion) something meaningful that they learned about their partner's culture, and about how their perception of the "other" or how their ways of interacting with others have changed over time.
6. At the end of the experience, domestic students are asked to reflect on the implications of the experience, paying particular attention to how this applied to their role as a teacher.

Following are a few sample statements from student experiences:

JP: Our conversations together have been more informative than any world history class I have ever taken.

RS: Spending time with my conversation partner has greatly affected the way I now view her. At first, I only saw her as a student coming from Japan. Now, I am able to see her as a 20-year-old female very similar to myself! By engaging in conversations, sharing meals together, and going places together, we have come to see the ways we are alike and the ways we are different. Although we may like different foods or look different from one another, we both have the same emotions. . . . This has created a bond between the two of us.

I would love to emulate this within my own classroom someday. Whether that be through Skype, e-mail, or field trips, I feel that showing students how similar they are to students across the globe, we will foster caring, loving, and understanding students. This may inspire them to study more about other cultures, or to even help solve global issues. I feel this has been very beneficial.

CS: I will not refer to anyone as my "global partners" since they are now my friends. My friends have taught me a lot about adjustment to life in the United States and how this applies to the lives of children and teachers in school today. . . . I know that I will now better understand the needs of children who may be struggling with their adjustment. . . . I think it is important for all teachers to seek opportunities to be around, work with, and learn from diverse groups of people.

SP: I have a better understanding of what is really going on with people who move to another country. At first, it seems like this person is really enjoying the new country that they are in, but this can change very quickly. Also, although it takes time for a person to really understand another culture and customs, that time will come.

There are a few things I, as a teacher, need to keep in mind. First, be patient. It is going to take time for a student to adjust to a new culture. . . . Let them know you are there for them and willing to help in any way. . . . Do your best to make them feel welcome and part of the class. . . . Although you think it may not help them adjust, it is a good idea to help them remember the culture they came from, . . . It is also important that the other students in the class understand this student's culture because it will also help them to adjust to the new student.

JB: My partner was curious to know what I was going to do for Thanksgiving, the kinds of foods I was going to eat, and who I was spending my holiday with. So I told her that I was going home for break, and I told her about traditional foods such as turkey, sweet potatoes, stuffing and pumpkin pie. She asked me, "Your family makes all of that every year?" It made me smile, but I said, yeah, we do it because it's part of our Thanksgiving tradition.

So then I asked her what she was doing during the break. She told me she was traveling to Chicago with some of her friends. She also told me she won't be going back to Tokyo until school is over in May. Then, it hit me. She is so far away from her family and friends and she will not be able to see them for almost an entire year. It made me feel sad because even though she has friends here, it's still not the same as being with the person that you have grown up with and love.

Thinking about that led me to think about children from other countries that might be in my classroom one day. There are some factors that are obvious, such as the language barrier. But I guess I never considered the emotional struggle of not being able to spend time with some family members and friends. Older people can deal with separation better than young children can. I just feel that as educators this is something we should keep in mind when we are teaching.

JW: It is amazing how much I have learned this semester about Turkey and the transition foreigners have to make when they come to the United States. Not only have I realized how stereotypical my thinking has been until I met my partner—the first Muslim I've ever met, but I also started to understand how difficult it is to make a transition into a new culture. I was anxious at the beginning of the experience, but I am glad the way it turned out. I feel silly for thinking that all Muslims were the same because I know that all white people or all Christians are not the same.

AH: When I first received this assignment, I was terrified to actually go through with it because I figured it would be so uncomfortable. I was worried that I would not be able to understand him, that I would not know what to talk about and if the whole experience would be awkward. What I did not realize at that time was that this must be how he feels every day coming to a new country where he never knows if he is going to understand what anyone is talking about, or if he will know what to say next.

At my first meeting, I at least told myself that it will be over in an hour or so, and then I can go back to my friends and to people that I am comfortable with. I now realize how selfish this thought was because he did not have that opportunity once he came to the United States.

REFERENCES

Cushner, K. (2007). The role of experience in the making of internationally-minded teachers. *Teacher Education Quarterly, 34*(1), 27–40.
Dunne, C. (2009). Host students' perspectives of intercultural contact in an Irish university. *Journal of Studies in International Education, 13*, 222–39.

Groeppel-Klein, A., Germelmann, C., & Glaum, M. (2010). Intercultural interaction needs more than mere exposure: Search for drivers of student interaction at border universities. *International Journal of Intercultural Relations, 34,* 253–67.

Halualani, R., Chitgopekar, A., Morrison, J., & Dodge, P. (2004). Who's interacting? And what are they talking about?—Intercultural contact and interaction among multicultural university students. *International Journal of Intercultural Relations, 28,* 353–72.

Hyde, C., & Ruth, B. (2002). Multicultural content and class participation: Do students self-censor? *Journal of Social Work Education, 38,* 241–56.

Le Roux, J. (2010). Social dynamics of the multicultural classroom. *Intercultural Education, 12,* 273–88.

Nesdale, D., & Todd, P. (1993). Internationalising Australian universities: The intercultural contact issue. *Journal of Tertiary Education Administration, 15,* 189–202.

Peacock, N., & Harrison, N. (2009). "It's so much easier to go with what's easy": 'Mindfulness' and the discourse between home and international students in the UK. *Journal of Studies in International Education, 13,* 487–508.

Sánchez, J. (2004). Intergroup perception of international students. *Academic Exchange Quarterly, 8,* 309–13.

Spencer-Rodgers, J. (2001). Consensual and individual stereotypic beliefs about international students among American host nationals. *International Journal of Intercultural Relations, 25,* 639–57.

Ward, C., Masgoret, A.-M., Ho, E., Holmes, P., Newton, J. & Crabbe, D. (2005). *Interactions with international students: Report prepared for Education New Zealand.* Wellington: Center for Applied Cross-cultural Research, Victoria University of Wellington.

Activity 10

The Intercultural Market: An Exercise in the Development of Cultural Intelligence

Keith Sakuda

ABSTRACT

Cultural intelligence is an alternative perspective to intercultural training's traditional focus on country-specific information and awareness of cross-cultural values and beliefs. By promoting intercultural knowledge, skills, and abilities that extend beyond specific countries, cultural intelligence training seeks to prepare individuals for interactions involving people from multiple countries and cultures. It also focuses attention on the often subtle aspects of cultural difference that may act to unconsciously limit people's ability to understand fully the communication messages being used by people from differing cultures.

The Intercultural Market Exercise creates an artificial cultural environment where participants can develop their cultural intelligence by testing their ability to interact with others from unfamiliar cultural backgrounds. To mimic the purpose-oriented nature of most international assignments in business, for instance, the activity includes a simulated buying and selling of food to force task-motivated interactions between participants.

BACKGROUND AND PURPOSE

The transition from international assignments to global assignments has created a need for intercultural training that extends beyond preparing people for assignments to a single specific country (Earley & Mosakowski, 2004). Global professionals find themselves traveling the world from country to country while interacting with a multitude of different cultures every day. For them, intercultural training must transcend the traditional boundaries of countries and their cultures.

Cultural intelligence is a framework for the development of knowledge, skills, and abilities for the global environment (Earley & Peterson, 2004). Borrowing from Gardner's (1983) theory of multiple intelligences, which inspired the concepts of emotional intelligence (Goleman, 1995) and social intelligence (Goleman, 2006), it refers to a person's ability to adapt effectively to new cultural environments (Earley & Ang, 2003). Consisting of the three elements of cognition, motivation, and behavior, it reflects the need for mental, physical, and emotional skills for interacting with new cultures (Earley & Mosakowski, 2004; Earley & Peterson, 2004).

Intercultural training is most effective when combining informational and experiential methods (Fowler & Blohm, 2004). For cultural intelligence, informational training typically includes both metacognitive and cognitive aspects (Tan & Chua, 2003). Metacognitive training focuses on the development of a mindset or cognitive strategy to effectively map out intercultural encounters. Cognitive training focuses on learning of cross-cultural theories and cultural knowledge that can aid in understanding or interpreting different cultural cues.

Experiential training, such as simulations and cross-cultural encounters, provides opportunities for emotional engagement essential to developing motivational and behavioral aspects of cultural intelligence (Tan & Chua, 2003). Direct experiences, even if done under tightly controlled environments, are able to provoke emotional responses to motivate participants to compare and contrast their values, beliefs, and cultural assumptions against other cultures. Such training also allows for participants to practice performing the physical acts and behaviors needed to seamlessly integrate into different cultures.

Existing intercultural simulations, such as BaFa' BaFa'™ (Shirts, 1974), have been successful in creating emotionally safe environments where participants are able to think about culture, cross-cultural differences, and cross-cultural behaviors. However, most overseas assignments are for professional or work-related purposes, not just cultural explorations. Most simulations' focus and emphasis on culture prevents them from properly mimicking the actual circumstances participants will experience in their global travels.

The purpose of this activity is to create an artificial intercultural environment where participants may test their cultural intelligence while exploring their ability to interpret and perform unfamiliar cultural behaviors. A mild level of cross-cultural conflict is designed into the activity to subject participants to motivational cultural intelligence stressors.

Unique to this simulation is the creation of an interactive marketplace for food. The buying and selling of food is intended to force participants to balance their attention to culture with a concern for a primary task. Participants who actively engage in the market must learn to prioritize and ration their attention between culture and work, adding a challenging twist to the simulation.

LEARNING OBJECTIVES

In this exercise, participants will:

- evaluate their level of intercultural skills through a simulated experience;
- demonstrate their cognitive/metacognitive cultural intelligence;
- demonstrate their physical cultural intelligence;
- demonstrate their motivational cultural intelligence;
- develop awareness of their personal biases towards different types of behaviors and attitudes;
- develop awareness of their personal assumptions about motivations and attitudes; and
- learn the difficulty of prioritizing intercultural awareness against other tasks.

PROCEDURE

Time Required: 30 minutes
Participants Needed: Recommended more than twelve participants and at least one facilitator. Simulation has been conducted in classes as large as forty participants.

1. Participants must be divided into three different Cultures: ALPHAN, BETAN, and OMEGAN. If the participant pool is large, each Culture may be further divided into two separate Clans. For example, Alpha-1 or Beta-2.
2. Each Culture should receive their respective Cultural Background Handout. Cultural Background Handouts describe each Culture and appropriate Cultural behaviors and attitudes. See Appendix A for Cultural Background Handouts.
3. If Cultures are separated into Clans, each Clan should receive their respective Clan Background Handout and appropriate supplies. Clan Background Handouts describe each Clan as well as their purposes and motivations for the simulation. See Appendix B for Clan Background Handouts. If Cultures are not divided into Clans, handouts for Alpha-1, Beta-1, and Omega-1 should be distributed as appropriate.
4. Each Culture/Clan should be given time to read their handouts and to practice their culturally appropriate behaviors and attitudes. At this time the facilitator(s) should assist any group in understanding their roles and responsibilities. Some clans may also need to discuss group strategies.

5. The facilitator(s) must confirm that all Cultures/Clans understand their roles and are able to perform any culturally appropriate behaviors.

6. Once the facilitator(s) has confirmed Step 5, Cultures/Clans should be allowed to engage in the market exchange of food for money. Throughout the activity, the facilitator(s) should constantly remind participants to remain in their cultural roles (behaviors, attitudes, motivations, etc.). The facilitator(s) should also repeatedly announce the importance of buying and selling food. For example, repeating the statement, "If you don't buy enough food, your family will starve."

7. The market exchange should last no longer than five minutes to promote a sense of urgency.

8. At the close of the market, participants should gather with their Culture/Clan to prepare for the debriefing.

DEBRIEFING THE ACTIVITY

The debriefing should begin with a general discussion of the activity. Broad questions such as "How was it?" or "What were your thoughts?" should be asked of the participants. During these discussions, the facilitator(s) should take note of repeated themes or any thoughts participants had about members of other Cultures/Clans. In particular, the following common themes are often mentioned:

- Success in accomplishing one's task (priority of task over intercultural awareness).
- Feelings of uneasiness or blatant dislike toward a certain Culture/Clan (personal biases toward behaviors or attitudes).
- Generalized feeling of discomfort or uneasiness (motivational cultural intelligence).

The second stage of the debriefing should ask for participants to describe the other Cultures/Clans. Questions such as, "What did you think about the Betans?" "Did anyone notice that the Alphans did something strange with their hands?" or "How did the Omegans make you feel?" should be asked of the participants. Don't forget to ask Clans of the same Culture to describe the other Clan.

The following questions can be focused around the different Cultures. ALPHAN:

1. Were you aware of their physical behaviors (hand gestures, speech patterns, etc.)? Did you notice any gender differences between males and females?

2. Were you willing and able to repeat the gestures? Did you have to consciously think about the behaviors, or did you naturally reflect

on their behaviors? Were you worried about making mistakes? Did they laugh at you if you made a mistake?

3. Were there differences between the two Alphan clans (if involved)?

BETAN:

1. How did your negotiations start? Did you approach them or did they approach you? Did you feel comfortable during your negotiations?

2. How did the Betans make you feel during your negotiations? What happened if you couldn't reach a price quickly?

OMEGAN:

1. Did any men approach an Omegan female? What was the reaction? Did any Betan approach an Omegan? What happened?

2. Did anyone feel they received special attention from the Omegans? Why?

3. What were the Omegans doing?

The third stage of the debriefing should ask participants to think about their personal approach to the marketplace and other Cultures/Clans. During this stage, participants should be asked about their mindset before engaging with other cultures. Questions such as "Did you have a business strategy for negotiating a price for food?" and "Did you have a cultural strategy for engaging the other culture?" should be asked. During this section of the debriefing, participants should be encouraged to think about metacognition in relation to intercultural experiences.

If participants have difficulty in describing the other Cultures/Clans, especially during the second stage of the debriefing, the facilitator(s) should initially emphasize that the activity is an intercultural simulation. Often, the pursuit of financial gains, or for some groups subsistence needs, may take priority over a participant's awareness of the intercultural context of the exercise.

On occasion a participant may respond defensively when asked to explain their lack of an intercultural focus during the activity. In such a situation the facilitator(s) should reassure the participant that the activity is designed to pull attention away from focusing only on culture. Real money, the sense of urgency to complete tasks, the emphasis on family need for food or the need for money, the short timeframe for the market, and the pursuit of love (or at least a mate) are all factors that are encountered during real intercultural experiences.

These distractions are designed to mimic real-life situations that often take priority over intercultural awareness during the course of international business, overseas adventure, or other international ventures. Participants can also consider the implications of this exercise in a nonbusiness setting. How might this inform teacher-parent relationships, for instance? Or student-student interactions?

REFERENCES

Earley, P. C., & Ang, S. (2003). *Cultural Intelligence: Individual Interactions across Cultures*. Stanford, CA: Stanford University Press.

Earley, P. C., & Mosakowski, E. (2004). Cultural intelligence. *Harvard Business Review, 82*(10), 139–46.

Earley, P. C., & Peterson, R. S. (2004). The elusive cultural chameleon: Cultural intelligence as a new approach to intercultural training for the global manager. *Academy of Management Learning and Education, 3*(1), 100–115.

Fowler, S. M., & Blohm, J. M. (2004). An analysis of methods for intercultural training. In D. Landis, J. M. Bennett, & M. J. Bennett (Eds.), *Handbook of intercultural training* (pp. 37–85). Thousand Oaks, CA: Sage.

Gardner, H. (1983). *Multiple Intelligences: The Theory in Practice*. New York: Basic Books.

Goleman, D. (1995). *Emotional Intelligence: Why It Can Matter More Than IQ*. New York: Bantam Books.

Goleman, D. (2006). *Social Intelligence: The New Science of Human Relationships*. New York: Bantam Books.

Shirts, R. G. (1974). *BaFa BaFa: A Cross-Cultural Simulation*. Del Mar, CA: Simile II.

Tan, J. S., & Chua, R. Y. J. (2003). Training and developing cultural intelligence. In P. C. Earley & S. Ang (Eds.), *Cultural Intelligence: Individual Interactions across Cultures* (pp. 258–303). Stanford, CA: Stanford University Press.

APPENDIX A

Culture Background Handouts

ALPHAN CULTURE	ALPHAN culture values adherence to traditions. The most important tradition is the use of hands when talking to people. When speaking, ALPHANS place a closed fist over their heart. ALPHANS signal that they are finished speaking by opening their fist while leaving their hand over their heart. This is important because ALPHANS speak in a very slow, deliberate manner. By watching an ALPHAN'S fist/open hand, one knows when they are done speaking. Men use their right hand, while women use their left hand. If a person uses the wrong hand, it probably means they are lost and confused. Feel free to laugh at them (but don't tell them why). Interrupting an ALPHAN while their fist is closed (speaking) is VERY rude. You wouldn't want to do business with a rude person.
BETAN CULTURE	BETANS are a very individualistic and very adventurous group of people. When speaking to people, BETANS tend to be very animated and use hand gestures and body language. BETANS also like to touch people gently on the shoulder when speaking to them because it shows a direct emotional link. BETANS tend to speak their minds and voice their own opinions freely, often interrupting when others are speaking. BETAN culture accepts such interruptions if one first raises their hand and offers an apology before beginning to speak. As long as someone raises their hand and apologizes, it's okay to interrupt. However, interrupting without raising one's hand and apologizing is VERY rude. You wouldn't want to do business with a rude person.
OMEGAN CULTURE	OMEGANS come from a very small island. Because of this, they are very distrusting of outsiders (non-OMEGANS). They tend to be a very quiet and reserved people. OMEGANS are suspicious when approached by people they don't know, but are willing to approach strangers to engage in commerce or trade. OMEGAN culture is very group oriented. They always do things as a group and have a very strict hierarchy of authority. Taller people have greater authority. Because a person's height is very important in OMEGAN culture, they always stand when meeting people. When speaking to others, OMEGANS prefer to sit so everyone is of a similar height. However, if a disagreement develops, OMEGANS will stand to emphasize their authority and status. When making decisions, OMEGANS will discuss things as a group; however the tallest person will make the final decision. If it is a group of men and women, the tallest woman has the authority to make final decisions. Women are very important in OMEGAN society, so OMEGAN men are very protective of OMEGAN women. Strangers, especially male strangers, should NEVER speak directly to an OMEGAN woman.

Table 10.1.

APPENDIX B

Clan Background Handouts

ALPHAN-1: Your clan needs money because the clan is in debt. If you don't make money, the clan will lose their farm. Each person is responsible for selling 5 units of food. The lowest price you are willing to sell at is \$0.03 a unit, but you would like to sell at a higher price. When negotiating, ALPHANS always start at a very high price and work down to a more realistic price. Supplies: each person should receive 5 units of a marker representing food (e.g. candies, poker chips, or small pieces of paper).	ALPHAN-2: Your clan had a very good harvest and wants to sell the clan's excess food. Each person is responsible for selling 5 units of food. Your primary goal is to sell all your food for as much money as you can. Your secondary goal is to outsell the other ALPHAN clan (rival clan). One strategy is to stay close to the other clan and sell your food to the people who are interested in buying food from them. It is important that they sell as little as possible. When negotiating, ALPHANS always start at a very high price and work down to more realistic price. Supplies: Each person should receive 5 units of a marker representing food (e.g. candies, poker chips, or small pieces of paper).
BETAN-1: Your family is starving! Clan affiliation means nothing if your family is hungry. You have \$0.25 to buy as much food as possible for your family (at least 5 units). If you don't buy food, your family will starve. Your family needs as much food as possible and there are many people selling food, so find the best price. Hurry! Supplies: Each person should receive \$0.25. If possible, include pennies and smaller denominations of coins.	BETAN-2: Your family is starving! Clan affiliation means nothing if your family is hungry. You have \$0.25 to buy as much food as possible for your family (at least 5 units). If you don't buy food, your family will starve. Your family needs as much food as possible and there are many people selling food, so find the best price. Hurry! Supplies: Each person should receive \$0.25. If possible, include pennies and smaller denominations of coins.
OMEGAN-1: Your Queen (tallest woman in the clan) needs a mate (must be a male), but clan tradition forbids her from mating with an OMEGAN. The buying and selling of food is just cover for finding a good mate for the Queen. The clan has \$1.00. Use the buying and selling of food to find a good mate for the Queen. The clan must decide what qualities to look for in a prospective mate for the Queen. Love is irrelevant. Do not tell people you are looking for a mate for the Queen. You may break up into smaller groups, but only if there are three or more people in each group. Remember, in OMEGAN culture the tallest person makes all final decisions. Supplies: The Clan should receive \$1.00. If possible, include pennies and smaller denominations of coins.	OMEGAN-2: Your clan desperately needs money. The clan has 30 units of food. Buy and sell with people outside of your clan to make as much money as possible. Clan tradition forbids buying or selling with other OMEGANS, so you must interact with the other cultures. You may break up into smaller groups, but only if there are three or more people in each group. Remember, in OMEGAN culture the tallest person makes all final decisions. Supplies: The Clan should receive 30 units of a marker representing food (e.g. candy, poker chips, or small pieces of paper).

Table 10.2.

Activity 11

What Lies at the Bottom ......????? An Inquiry-Based Nature of Science (NOS) Activity with a Multicultural Twist

Rajlakshmi Ghosh

ABSTRACT

Scientific inquiry and nature of science (NOS) are two essential components that create a meaningful foundation for authentic learning of science content and concepts by assisting students to explore the variety of ways scientific knowledge develops and how it is different from other disciplines. An important tenet of NOS includes recognizing the socially and culturally embedded nature of science. Exploring this tenet with students can make cultural diversity better accepted and appreciated in today's multicultural classrooms.

The following activity, "What Lies at the Bottom?" is an inquiry-based activity that is designed to teach NOS aspects in the middle-grade science classroom, and at the same time to teach the appreciation of the culturally embedded nature of scientific knowledge. The activity is designed to assist a middle school science teacher to "walk the talk" as indicated by Edwards and Kuhlman (2007).

The activity teaches some of the major aspects of NOS—namely tentativeness, subjectivity in science, and the role of observation and inference and considers the notion that there really is no single universally accepted scientific method—that social and cultural contexts have an influence by letting the students experience them using scientific inquiry. By crafting NOS instruction to reflect cultural particulars relevant to the background of the students in the classroom, this activity aims to engage students in exploring NOS aspects and accomplish science learning often in ways that link to their personal interests, thus rendering it meaningful.

BACKGROUND AND PURPOSE

Nature of Science (NOS) refers to the values and beliefs that are inherent to scientific knowledge and the epistemology of scientific thinking (Lederman, 1992). Some of the key tenets of NOS include understanding that scientific knowledge is empirical, tentative, and subjective; that it is based on observations and inference; that there is a role for creativity and imagination in science; that theory and laws are different; that there is no single scientific method; and that science is socially and culturally embedded.

Scientific inquiry is often defined as an active learning process in which students answer questions through their own investigations and data analysis (Bell, Smetana, & Binns, 2005). Both inquiry-based science teaching and NOS have been strongly recommended by the National Science Education Standards and Benchmarks (American Association for the Advancement of Science [AAAS], 1993; National Research Council [NRC], 1996, 2012) with an aim to provide all students with equal opportunity to learn science concepts and processes and to understand how scientists study the world around them.

Explicit NOS instruction often addresses misconceptions in science that may be held by teachers and students (Abd-El-Khalick & Akerson, 2004; Abd-El-Khalick & Lederman, 2000; Akerson, Abd-El-Khalick, & Lederman 2000; Khishfe & Lederman 2007; Seung, Bryan, & Butler, 2009). Particularly, the sociocultural aspect of NOS is deeply emphasized by the Next Generation Science Standards (NGSS) (NRC, 2012), which views science learning as a cultural accomplishment. The standards recognize culturally responsive science teaching as strategies that involve recognition of the community practices around scientific endeavors (NRC, 2012).

The following is one such activity that integrates aspects of NOS instruction and culturally responsive teaching. The purpose of this activity is to help students accomplish an understanding of key aspects of NOS and at the same time experience one of the key NOS tenets—that scientific knowledge is socially and culturally embedded. Thus, students develop science-linked identities by realizing that science could be meaningfully related to circumstances of their own lives, and that would make NOS learning engaging and meaningful.

LEARNING OBJECTIVES

Through this activity, the students will be able to achieve the following *science process skills*:

- identifying questions that can be answered through scientific investigations;
- designing and conducting a scientific investigation;

- using appropriate mathematics, tools, and techniques to gather data and information;
- analyzing and interpreting data;
- developing descriptions, models, explanations, and predictions;
- thinking critically and logically to connect evidence and explanations;
- recognizing and analyzing alternative explanations and predictions; and
- communicating scientific procedures and explanations.

In addition, through this activity students would be able to experience the following tenets of nature of science:

- that the tentative nature of science—scientific knowledge is subject to change. Our background knowledge influences our inferences.
- that subjectivity may be operating—an individual's background knowledge and scientific conceptual framework impact how one observes, perceives. and interprets data.
- that there is no single scientific method—science employs multiple methods. The commonly seen 5-Step or 7-Step Scientific Method presented in textbooks is a myth; it outlines just *one* example of the many methods employed by scientists.
- that science is socially and culturally embedded. Scientific knowledge is developed within a particular social and cultural context, reflecting the prevailing thinking of the historical perspective, its geographical location, and its cultural milieu. All these impact the questions pursued by scientists, the methods they employ, the interpretation of data, and the reporting of findings.

MATERIALS NEEDED

Precut paper that can be folded and taped to form cubes, tape, and scissors. See figures at the end of the chapter for outline details.

PROCEDURE

(total time—approximately 40 minutes)

Step 1: Students study cubes with English numbers 1–6 (5 minutes).

The original idea for this lesson stems from an activity in *Teaching about Evolution and the Nature of Science* published by the National Academy of Sciences (1998). The activity begins with a paper cube with numbers 1–6 as on dice (see figure 11.1 for the outline of the paper that can be cut, folded, and taped to form the cube) that will be placed in front of students. Instructors ask a question: "What do you think lies at the bottom?" Students have to investigate the answer without touching the cube. Ideally, students would observe, identify a pattern, and come to a conclusion about what number lies at the bottom. Each group would be asked to share their findings. Teachers debrief, linking the activity to NOS as indicated in the following section.

Debriefing: Discussing the tentative nature of science, no single method (ten minutes). Teachers can talk about a few key components of NOS while discussing their students' findings. The first could be the tentative nature of science. When teachers ask the students how they came to a conclusion and how sure they are about their claims, students should be able to justify their answers by providing a possible explanation of the methods they used.

Teachers can discuss that the findings were based on observation and inferences that were influenced by their background knowledge, in this case, their knowledge of the English numbers. It is their prior knowledge that assisted them to come to a conclusion that they are sure of. Instructors can explain the tentative nature of science and emphasize that the bottom number could be anything.

One group can have a blank face instead of a number to emphasize that point. Teachers can also demonstrate that there is no single way of coming to a conclusion. Students can discuss the methods they used to find the answer. They can observe the pattern of increase in numbers from 1 through 6, or infer that opposite sides add up to 7. Through this, students can explore that science also employs multiple methods similar to how they did it. The commonly seen 5-Step or 7-Step Scientific Method presented in textbooks is a myth as it outlines just *one of the many* methods employed by scientists.

Step 2: Students exploring Spanish or Hindi number cubes (10 minutes).

In adding an intercultural element to the activity, we would introduce two other versions of the cubes, one with numbers spelled in Spanish (1 through 6) and one with Hindi numbers (see figures 11.2 and 11.3 for outlines). Again, teachers ask students to find out what lies at the bottom by observing the visible sides only.

Debriefing: Science is socially and culturally embedded (5 minutes). Depending on their knowledge of the foreign language, students may or may not come up with the answer. We can explain again that prior knowledge or background knowledge plays a role in doing science. We use our background knowledge (what we know) to make sense of our observations (interpret what we see).

In this case, prior knowledge of the particular foreign language was essential to obtaining the correct answer in this activity, indicating that science is also socially and culturally embedded. Because Spanish is a common language in the United States, many students would have the knowledge of Spanish numbers and will get the right answer. Teachers can explain that scientific knowledge is not only based on observation and inferences, but is also developed within a particular social and cultural context (in this case, the knowledge of Spanish numbers). All the aspects experienced in this part of the activity also mirror the ways scientists explore the natural world.

Step 3: Making your own puzzle (5 minutes).

For the final part, teachers give students blank cubes (see figure 11.4), where they will be asked to design their own puzzle, which they let their fellow students solve with the same question: "What lies at the bottom?"

Debriefing: Science is socially and culturally embedded (5 minutes). It would be interesting to see how the puzzles that students design reflect their own sociocultural background. Teachers, once again, may discuss the socially and culturally reflective nature of science. This activity has been tried with students from India, the Philippines, Saudi Arabia, and Kenya in a mixed classroom along with U.S. students. Most of the time, the puzzles developed by the students reflected their cultural thinking in some ways.

The Bottom Line (Conclusion): Tying to Content (5 minutes).

Students would reflect on the key tenets of NOS as experienced by their solving the cubes puzzle. Teachers can explain how science processes and NOS aspects influence the work of scientists. In other words, teachers can discuss related science content about how scientists work using the learning obtained from this cubes activity.

It is important for the students to know that the process skills as explored in this activity are also the same process skills used by scientists to explore the natural world. Examples in this regard are the discovery of the structure of DNA, the re-creation of organisms from fossil records, the discovery of atomic structure, and the tracing of the origin of early man. Teachers can explain that all these scientific explorations, and many others, used some sort of NOS understandings, including the ones explored by this session. This activity could be a precursor to any of the aforementioned science content lessons. The key idea is to emphasize the key NOS tenets, explore multiculturalism, and experience how these tenets affect a generation of scientific knowledge.

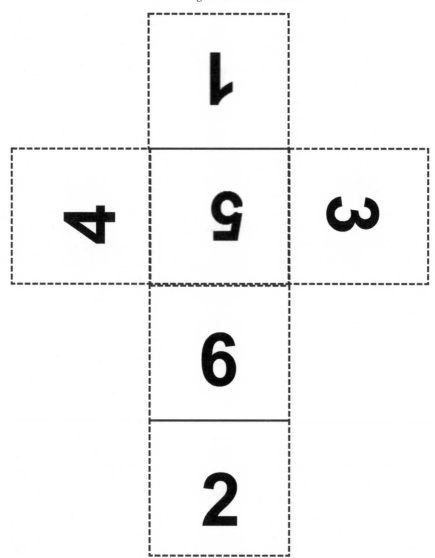

Figure 11.1

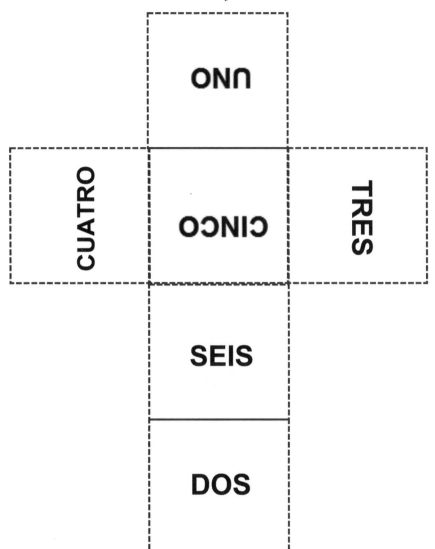

Figure 11.2

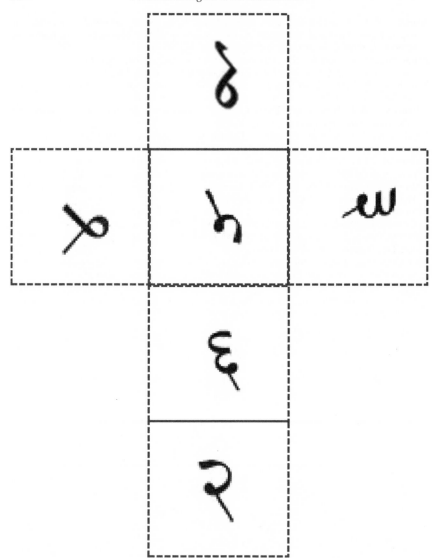

Figure 11.3

REFERENCES

Abd-El-Khalick, F., & Akerson, V. L. (2004). Learning about nature of science as conceptual change: Factors that mediate the development of preservice elementary teachers' views of nature of science. *Science Education, 88,* 785–810.

Abd-El-Khalick, F., & Lederman, N. G. (2000). Improving science teachers' conceptions of the nature of science: A critical review of the literature. *International Journal of Science Education, 22,* 665–701.

Akerson, V. L., Abd-El-Khalick, F., & Lederman, N. G. (2000). Influence of a reflective explicit activity based approach on elementary teachers' conceptions of nature of science. *Journal of Research in Science Teaching, 37*, 295–317.

American Association for the Advancement of Science. (1993). *Benchmarks for science literacy: A Project 2061 report*. New York: Oxford University Press.

Bell, R. L., Smetana, L. & Binns, I. (2005). Simplifying inquiry instruction. *Science Teacher, 72*(7), 30–33.

Edwards, S. & Kuhlman, W. (2007). Culturally responsive teaching: Do we walk our talk? *Multicultural Education, 14*(4), 45–51.

Khishfe, R., & Lederman, N. (2007). Relationship between instructional context and views of nature of science. *International Journal of Science Education, 29*, 939–61.

Lederman, N. G. (1992). Students' and teachers' conceptions of the nature of science: A review of the research. *Journal of Research in Science Teaching, 29*(4), 331–59.

National Academy of Sciences (1998). *Teaching about Evolution and the Nature of Science*. Washington, DC: National Academy Press.

National Research Council. (2012). *A Framework for K–12 Science Education: Practices, Crosscutting Concepts and Core Ideas*. Washington, DC: National Academy Press.

National Research Council. (1996). National Science Education Standards. Washington, DC: National Academy Press.

Ohio Department of Education. (2012). *Ohio revised science standards and model curriculum for grades K through Eight*. Retrieved from http://www.ode.state.oh.us/.

Seung, E., Bryan, L., & Butler, M. (2009). Improving preservice middle grades science teachers' understanding of the nature of science using three instructional approaches. *Journal of Science Teacher Education, 20*, 157–77.

Activity 12

Sexuality, Gender, and Families in the Animal Kingdom:
Lessons from the Wild

Sara Raven

ABSTRACT

Sexuality and gender can be difficult concepts to discuss in everyday life, let alone in the science classroom with young people. Additionally, science lessons that confront normative issues to promote equity are rare. This lesson provides an opportunity for teachers and students in science classrooms to have a lesson about the animal kingdom and to examine the tangential issues associated with these concepts. Students will examine sexuality, gender, and family structures in various animal species.

Reasons for this lesson are twofold. One, students will build their knowledge of the animal kingdom, sexual reproduction, and animal behavior. Two, students will be able to use this knowledge to examine equity issues related to sexuality and gender, different cultures' perceptions of sexuality and gender, and the nature of science as social knowledge.

BACKGROUND AND PURPOSE

Incorporating social and cultural issues into the science classroom can be a challenge. More often than not, if and when attempted, social and multicultural issues in science are presented in a rather traditional manner in what I refer to as curriculum "add-ons." These add-ons typically introduce multicultural aspects of science by introducing such aspects as female and nonwhite scientists or indigenous science knowledge.

This method of multicultural science is effective, as science education that focuses on the norms of a single culture, despite a multicultural reality, is an education system that fosters discrimination, bias, and a misunderstanding of science (Atwater & Riley, 1993). This type of lesson, however, is not what I present here. Rather, I present a science lesson plan that originates in a place of equity and diversity. Moore (2008) described this as a type of science that "create[s] science classroom communities with access, equity, quality, and opportunity to learn science as fundamental goals" (p. 591).

This lesson provides an opportunity for science teachers and students to examine the construction of social hierarchies and their relation to science. This exploration of inequity involves "the deconstruction of unjust and oppressive structures" (Lewis, 2001, p. 189). The activity that follows can be used to introduce high school science students to the various kinds of family structures in the animal kingdom. It is designed to explore some of the social biases that surround families and sexuality in human culture and provide a counterpoint to these biases.

Students will learn about sexual reproduction and family structures of various animal species and begin a discourse on these structures and how they relate to human culture. Additionally, students will understand that science is not apolitical or asocial and will expand their understandings of the nature of science. Finally, students will learn more about how different cultures view sexuality and gender.

LEARNING OBJECTIVES

Although human anatomy is no longer a part of high school science standards, students are still expected to understand the animal kingdom and the types of reproduction used by various species of animals. Unfortunately, this instruction tends to be limited to discussions of sexual versus asexual reproduction, with no mention of different types of sexual reproduction or the family structures that animals have after reproduction has occurred. This activity gives students the opportunity to learn about the different types of sexual reproduction, gender differences, and family structures in the animal kingdom in the context of science education, as well as opening a discussion on sexuality and gender identity and equity in the classroom.

In this activity, students will:

1. learn about different types of sexual reproduction, gender differences, and family structures of various animal species;
2. learn about and be able to provide examples of sexuality and gender from different human cultures;
3. discuss issues of equity pertaining to sexuality and gender; and
4. reexamine the nature of science.

PROCEDURE

1. Lead the class in a discussion about the difference between asexual and sexual reproduction. Have students share their ideas about sexuality and family structures found in the animal kingdom.
2. Provide students with a copy of the chart at the end of the chapter (table 12.1). In it are the sexualities and family structures of nine different species of animal.
3. Separate students into groups of three or four students and have them discuss each species in terms of sexuality, gender, and family.
4. Have each group share their thoughts with the class. Make sure to leave time for questions.
5. The assignment for this lesson is individual. Each student will research one additional species of animal and provide information about the sexuality, gender, and family structure in that species.
6. As an additional piece to this lesson, students can go beyond the animal kingdom to research how human cultures view sexuality, gender, and family.
7. An additional piece to this lesson involves a discussion on the nature of science. Ask students about their conceptions of science and why they may not have heard this information before. One can also delve into the nature of scientific knowledge and consider why some types of science are more appropriate than others. For example, teachers can lead students in a discussion of the types of science investigations that are funded or the role of indigenous science knowledge.
8. Final note: Please be aware that discussions about sexuality, gender, families, and the nature of science can be sensitive. As the teacher, you should make every effort to ensure that your classroom is a safe space, and that students feel comfortable sharing their opinions and expressing their views openly. Additionally, discussions such as these can bring up very personal feelings and experiences, both on the part of the teacher and the students. Be sure to maintain a close watch on the discussion, stepping in when you are needed to support a safe and respectful learning environment.

Animal	Sexuality and Family Structure
Birds of paradise	Males are more colorful than the females, and must perform elaborate dances to convince females to mate.
Bonobo apes	Females, although weaker, rule the males using sex as a method of control. In this species, occurrences of homosexuality are very common. Sex, rather than violence, is used to resolve issues.
Discus fish	Males and females form monogamous pairs. The female guards her eggs, while the male guards her. After the eggs hatch, both male and female parents feed their young with a milky secretion from their skin.
Penguins	Homosexual penguins are not uncommon. This is not limited to any one species of penguin, either. Perhaps the most well-known example of this involves two penguins named Roy and Silo, a pair of male chinstrap penguins, who hatched and fostered a female chick from an egg they had been given.
Ruff birds	Males in this species use displaying behavior more with other males than females to establish a hierarchy. There are three different types of males: territorial, satellite, and faeder. The territorial male is strong, aggressive, and spends the majority of his time fighting other males. The satellite male is less muscular than the territorial male and is lighter in color. He sneak-breeds with other females, yet the territorial male tolerates this, since the presence of a satellite male attracts more females. Lastly, the faeder male is the smallest male type and looks more feminine. He sneak-breeds with other females, but will also mate with other males. This type of activity also attracts females.
Seahorses	In this species, females have a penis-like organ that they use to deposit eggs into the male's egg pouch. The males then fertilize the eggs and get pregnant, while the female begins to create more eggs.
Side-blotched lizards	Three different types of males exist in this species, each of which uses different tactics to mate with females. The orange-throated male is the largest, has the largest territory, and tries to mate with as many females as possible. However, because his territory is so large, he does not form strong bonds with the females. The blue-throated male is smaller and has a territory only big enough for one female. The yellow-throated male, however, is the smallest and most closely resembles the females. He stays at the outskirts of the orange-throated male's territory and mates with the females there, rather than finding others to mate with.
Spotted hyenas	Females of this species are much larger and more aggressive than the males. The females also have penises that are used to dominate the males by making mating difficult.
Tamarins	Families in this species include many different combinations, such as one male and two females, one male and one female, or one female and two males. The latter combination is the most common, as females usually give birth to twins, which are then cared for by the males.

Table 12.1

REFERENCES

Atwater, M. M., & Riley, J. P. (1993). Multicultural science education: Perspectives, definitions, and research agenda. *Science Education, 77*(6), 661–68.

Lewis, J. B. (2001, September/October). Social justice, social studies, social foundations. *The Social Studies,* 189–92.

Moore, F. M. (2008). Agency, identity, and social justice education: Preservice teachers' thoughts on becoming agents of change in urban elementary science classrooms. *Research in Science Education, 38,* 589–610.

Section 2

Addressing Social Justice through Social Foundations of Education

A rose in the desert

Marti'n
Marti'n de Porres
Son of mother Anna Vela'zquez
slave
Son of father Don Juan de Porres
conqueror
Brother of Juana
sister

Father of the slave boys
Father of the cirujanos
Father of the priests
Father of the sick
Father of the oppressed

No slave
this son of a Spanish conqueror
child of a Black Woman
not just a cleaner
not just a washer
a grower of lemons
a healer
of humans
and clothes
and animals

Saint
natural healer
longing to ease
the pain
of being
poor
Indian
Black
Despised

Rose
of the
desert
in
Lima
Patron saint
of the
poor
sickly
lost
oppressed
and
animals

Not a
slave
Not a
cleaner
Not a
hermano del barrio
our brother,
a
Rose.

—Joanne Kilgour Dowdy

Activity 13

Critically Examining Gender Roles: Deconstructing the Myth of "Boys Will Be Boys, Girls Will Be Girls"

Alyse C. Hachey and Yolanda Medina

Gender is between your ears and not between your legs.
— Chastity Bono

ABSTRACT

The baby comes out, genitalia are examined, and the baby is designated "boy" or "girl." With this, the child is assigned not only a sex, but by default, a corresponding gender role. Gender roles are a set of expectations regarding which behaviors are "appropriate" for a person's sex (Cahill & Adams, 1997).

Typically, gender roles are conceived in terms of dichotomous categories (man/woman), with mutually exclusive attributes. However, such a narrow view does not allow for the myriad of possible expressions of one's authentic, individual gender identity and the roles a person can enact within that identity (Ehrensaft, 2011). Further, stereotypical conceptions of gender provide the basis for bigotry, hatred, and violence against those perceived to not fit gender-role norms.

BACKGROUND AND PURPOSE

The critical issue for teaching is that gender roles are transmitted to children via social interaction; Menvielle (2011) holds that gender is "no more and no less than a creative, individual achievement, and yet it can only develop through social exchange" (p. xi). The minute the baby is wrapped in a blue blanket or a pink blanket, regardless of the sex of the child underneath, adult expectations and social responses are driven by the gender label and associated stereotypical attributes connected to the blanket color, rather than to the child himself or herself (Seavey, Katz & Zalk, 1975; Sidorowicz & Lunney, 1980). These adult social cues are then internalized by the child and serve to reinforce normative ways of being that may or may not mesh with the authentic self.

Later in the child's life, classroom materials, curriculum decisions, and ways of structuring social interaction, all dictated by the teacher, become the metaphorical blanket that wraps the child and serves to develop and strengthen conceptions of gender (Cahill & Theilheimer, 1999; Phillips, 2010). Research suggests that teachers often use gender role stereotypes to guide their interactions with young children. Furthermore, it shows that teachers become uncomfortable with children who act in ways counter to gender-role expectations and tend to squash such behavior.

This lack of comfort of cross-gender behavior has been linked to homophobic feelings in teachers (Cahill & Adams, 1997; Cahill & Theilheimer, 1999). What is often unrecognized and needs closer examination by pre-service and practicing teachers is that the stereotypical attributes associated and reinforced within gender roles are frequently counter to reality; for example, research shows that *gentleness* is as often a characteristic of males as females, even though it is not labeled as masculine (Phillips, 2010).

Erhensaft (2011) called this "blurring the line." We call it "living in the middle." Either way, the idea is that there is no "boys will be boys" and "girls will be girls" but instead, that a person's gender role is a mixture of socially constructed male and female attributes that serve to benefit and authenticate the individual self.

The purpose of this activity is to critically explore conceptions of gender roles and how such conceptions perpetuate stereotyped expectations of people that can lead to inequity, and even violence. Furthermore, this activity links conceptions of gender with teaching practice to highlight the function of teachers in socializing children toward/against normative gender roles.

LEARNING OBJECTIVES

This activity will enable practicing and pre-service teachers to:

- evaluate how issues of gender affect educational equity and success in America's schools and identify educational practices that minimize those effects;
- examine the role that teachers play in socializing children toward/ against gender-role norms and of adopting cross-gender attributes;
- evaluate the correlation between stereotypical gender-role expectations and homophobia and bullying; and
- critically question underlying assumptions and ideologies about society and schooling.

PROCEDURES

1. Have the students take out a piece of paper. Tell them "You have one minute to write down on the left side of your paper every word you can think of that describes a MAN." Give them the minute (or a bit longer if students are still writing). Then, tell the students: "You have one minute to write down on the right side of your paper every word you can think of that describes a WOMAN." Note: you can use MAN/WOMAN, MALE/FEMALE, or BOY/GIRL as the dichotomous gender labels since resulting attribute descriptors tend to be similar.

2. After students have individually completed their lists, divide a blackboard or whiteboard in half with the heading "MAN" on one side and the heading "WOMAN" on the other.

3. As a whole class, invite students to provide what they have written down for each gender until the two sides of the board are filled with student-generated attributes for each gender. Note: as the instructor, you may need to serve as editor while creating the whole-class gender lists; the point of this part of the activity is to end up with a large list of *generally* accepted expected/stereotypical gender attributes and your professional judgment will need to come into play to weed out student-provided attributes that you do not feel are general enough or are based on individual negative emotional responses.

   For instance, you may get for MAN an attribute of cheater; ask the students, "Do we expect all men to be cheaters?" Or for WOMAN, you may get an attribute of liar; ask the students "Do we expect all women to be liars?" The use of such questioning can allow the class to critically discuss/self-edit any attributes that you feel are questionable.

4. Invite the class to look at the list they have created and give the students a few minutes to read through it.

5. Ask the men in the class how many of them have some attributes listed on the WOMAN side of the list. Then ask the women how many of them have a few attributes listed on the MAN side of the list. Continue the discussion by asking the students which attributes they have from the opposite gender list (i.e., Alejandro, you said you have at least five from the WOMAN list, which ones? . . . tell us about that. Why do you take on these attributes? Rachel, explain the ones you have from the MAN list. What do you benefit from having these attributes?).

   Give the students enough time to share and personalize their cross-gender attributes. Then, ask the students: what would happen if this wasn't the case—if you men had only MAN attributes and you women had only the WOMAN attributes? Would this be beneficial to you? Would this be beneficial for society? Engage in a whole-class discussion until the critical conclusion is made: Adopting opposite gender attributes is beneficial for the individual and society.

6. Then ask the students what this means; if these attributes are MAN and these attributes are WOMAN, why do you have some from the opposite list? Is it really true that "boys will be boys, girls will be girls?" Engage in a whole-class discussion until the critical conclusion is made: Students do not exclusively belong to one list or the other regardless of their actual gender, and in fact, everyone has attributes from both gender role lists and it is in the middle of these two lists that we all find who we truly are.

7. Tell the students to now place themselves as a teacher in a classroom. Provide any or all of the following scenarios as provocation for discussion:

    - What is your reaction to the boy in your class who every day puts on a pink dressy skirt and plays with the baby dolls? Or to the boy who only wants to play in the kitchen area?
    - What is your reaction to the girl who only wants to play tackle football with the boys during recess?
    - What is your reaction when two boys, who as best friends, announce that they will get married when they grow up?
    - What is your reaction to the girl who plays combat with soldier and X-man figures and hates baby dolls because she adamantly states, "when I grow up, I am not going to have children . . . I am going to kill the bad guys and lead the army"?

    Engage in an open discussion of student reactions to such situations; as the instructor, highlight when students rely on arguments that are based on gender role stereotypes, referring back to the previous conversation about everyone having attributes from both lists. The impact of media/television and of classroom cultural artifacts (books, toys, technology, etc.) on conceptions of gender may also be introduced during the discussion. You can guide the conversation to address any/all of these underlying ideas: freedom of expression, fairness, sexuality, masculinity vs. femininity, individuality, tradition, creativity, continuity vs. change, pleasure and renunciation, bullying/social pressure.

8. Then, tell the students: We have established that you all enact attributes from the opposite gender list and that this can be positive/beneficial to you and society; yet, what do we call a man who has female attributes? (He must be gay, queer, fag, woosy, wimp, and a pussy); and what do we call a woman who has masculine attributes? (She must be a lesbian, dike, and a butch). Share the quote:

"People don't get beat up because they are gay, they get beat up because they look gay" (Medina, 2013). Ask the students, based on the recent conversation, what this quote means, Follow up by asking:

- How are stereotypical expectations of gender contributing to homophobia and bullying?
- What role do you as a teacher who socializes children play in perpetuating gender stereotypes?
- How can you as a teacher support children to develop individually authentic senses of gender?

Engage the students in an open discussion until the critical conclusion is made: Teachers play a role in socializing children either into or against stereotypical general roles. Reinforcing gender stereotypes is not beneficial to individual children or society; it perpetuates fear and inequality.

9. At the conclusion of this activity, have the students read an article or two from the suggested reading list. In addition, students can complete one or both of the suggested follow-up assignments. At the next class meeting, invite students to share any additional thoughts on the MAN/WOMAN activity, the content of the readings, and/or the follow-up assignments.

SUGGESTED READING LIST

Adler, P. A., Kless, S. J., & Adler, P. (1992). Socialization to gender roles: Popularity among elementary boys and girls. *Sociology in Education, 65*(3), 169–87.

Cahill, B., & Adams, E. (1997). An exploratory study of early childhood teacher's attitudes toward gender roles. *Sex Roles, 36*(7/8), 517–29.

Cahill, B. J., & Theilheimer, R. (1999). Can Tommy and Sam get married? Questions about gender, sexuality and young children. *Young Children, 54*(1), 27–31.

Carlson, D. (2012). *The Education of Eros: A History of Education and the Problem of Adolescent Sexuality.* New York: Routledge.

Carlson, D., & Roseboro, D. (2011). *The Sexuality Curriculum and Youth Culture.* New York: Peter Lang.

Ehrensaft, D. (2011). *Gender Born, Gender Made: Raising Healthy Gender Non-Conforming Children.* New York: Workman.

Gray, E. (2010). The culture of separate desks. In Y. Medina (Ed.), *Schooling in a Diverse American Society* (pp. 163–68). New York: Pearson Learning Solutions.

Jones, S., & Myhill, D. (2004). 'Troublesome boys' and 'compliant girls': Gender identity and perceptions of achievement and underachievement. *British Journal of Sociology of Education, 25*(5), 547–61.

Kimmel, M. (2010). What about the boys? In Y. Medina (Ed.), *Schooling in a diverse American society* (pp. 177–81). New York: Pearson Learning Solutions.

McGee, S. (2002). *Gender in Education. Reader.* San Francisco: Jossey-Bass.

Phillips, A. (2010). In the beginning they were babies. In Y. Medina (Ed.), *Schooling in a Diverse American Society* (pp. 163–75). New York: Pearson Learning Solutions.

Risner, D. (2010). What Mathew Sheppard would tell us: Gay and lesbian issues in education. In Y. Medina (Ed.), *Schooling in a Diverse American Society* (p. 183). New York: Pearson Learning Solutions.

Sadker, D., & Zittleman, K. (2009). *Still Failing at Fairness: How Gender Bias Cheats Girls and Boys in School and What We Can Do about It.* New York: Scribner.

SUGGESTED FOLLOW-UP ASSIGNMENTS

1. Provide the students with the lyrics to Beyonce Knowles's song "If I were a boy" (lyrics are available via an Internet search). Have students analyze the lyrics for stereotypical gender attributes (similar to the class activity, putting lyrics under "GIRL/BOY" categories and naming the related stereotypical gender role attribute). Then, have students write responses that draw from the class activity, readings, and personal experience to answer: How do songs and other media contribute to gender role stereotyping? What can you in your teaching practice do to counteract/protect against gender-role stereotypical messages?

2. Using any or all of the quotes below (or find your own), have students write responses that draw from the class activity, readings, and personal experience to relate the quote to ideas of teaching and gender-role socialization: What does this quote mean to you? What does this quote mean for teaching away from gender stereotypes?

    "Gender is between your ears and not between your legs." (Chastity Bono)

    "We've begun to raise daughters more like sons . . . but few have the courage to raise our sons more like our daughters." (Gloria Steinem)

    "How important it is for us to recognize and celebrate our heroes and she-roes!" (Maya Angelou)

    "Society tells a man: You are a Warrior, the world is yours to Conquer. But never prepares him for 'fall-back' action when that fails." "Society tells the woman: You are a Peacemaker. The World is your home, build and keep it Safe. Yet rejects her when she takes Action in War time to Protect, Preserve and Provide for her Home." (Eresi Ann Uduka)

    "Within the universe of the extraordinary, those qualities we designate to human concepts of gender are often shared, exchanged, or even completely obliterated. Because of this mixture of traits, these twins called Genius and Madness often appear to be the same thing. They both have a tendency to blur the lines of what we call norms, or established reality." (Aberjhani)

REFERENCES (NOT CITED IN THE SUGGESTED READING LIST)

Medina, Y. (2013). Personal lecture notes.

Menvielle, E. (2011). Forward. In D. Ehrensaft (Ed.), *Gender Born, Gender Made: Raising Healthy Gender Non-Conforming Children* (pp. ix–xi). New York: Workman.

Seavey, C., Katz, P., & Zalk, S. (1975). Baby X: The effect of gender labels on adult responses to infants. *Sex Roles, 1,* 103–9.

Sidorowicz, L. S., & Lunney, G. S. (1980). Baby X Revisited. *Sex Roles, 6*(1), 67–73.

Activity 14

When I Grow Up, I'll Work in the Factory Just Like My Daddy: Examining Teaching Practices That Perpetuate the Social Class Status Quo

Yolanda Medina and Alyse C. Hachey

I believe that to educate is a political act, one that can be used to both "maintain the status quo" and perpetuate social inequalities in a world seen as fixed, unchangeable, and taken for granted. On the other hand, we can educate to challenge the status quo by encouraging critical thinking and the questioning of the world.

—Peter McLaren, 2003

ABSTRACT

This activity is designed to help practicing and pre-service teachers develop an understanding of how teachers' assumptions of children based on their SES (socioeconomic status) can perpetuate social class inequities that will affect children for the rest of their lives. It aims to create awareness in teachers of the kinds of educational sensitivities needed to empower all children and to create social change.

BACKGROUND AND PURPOSE

Patrick Finn (2009), borrowing from Jean Anyon's (1980) research, argued that public schools generally provide the form of literacy instruction that prepares children for occupations similar to those of their parents. Thus, children from working class backgrounds are given literacy instruction needed to become complacent and unquestioning workers ready for manual labor and retail. Meanwhile, children from affluent communities are taught in ways that support the development of creativity and the leadership skills needed for such careers as artists, intellectuals, and CEOs of major corporations. In this way, socioeconomic status (also commonly referred to as social class) is preserved and social class inequity is perpetuated.

Finn (2009) demonstrated how in working class schools, and somewhat in middle class schools, teaching and learning is textbook driven, rote, hierarchical, and lacking connections to real life situations. Children in these schools receive the type of schooling that Paulo Freire (2000) coined the "banking concept of education" where learning is disconnected from all social relevance, knowledge is set by outside authorities, and the role of students is limited to collecting irrelevant information until the time comes that it is needed for a test. Freire argued that, "the more students work at storing the deposits entrusted to them, the less they develop the critical consciousness which would result from their intervention in the world as transformers of that world" (p. 74).

Furthermore, the structure of these schools is highly authoritarian; children are not allowed to get up from their seats and move around inside or outside the classroom unless permitted. Thus, working class children learn to see the world as set and unchangeable, and they begin to see themselves as people to whom things happen, not as people who make things happen. Needless to say, the academic expectations and social mobility of these children are close to nil.

In the wealthier schools, comprised of what Anyon (1980) termed "affluent professional and executive elite," creativity and individual growth are values at the forefront of every classroom. Teachers encourage students to think for themselves and come up with multiple ways of solving problems. The learning is relevant and children are able to constantly make connections between their lives and what they are learning in school. Children in these schools receive the type of education that empowers them to conquer the world, or at least to be able to manipulate it. This is an education comparable to Freire's "problem posing method" where students

> develop their power to perceive critically the way they exist in the world with which and in which they find themselves; they come to see the world not as a static reality, but as a reality in the process, in transformation. (Freire, 2000, p. 83)

Moreover, the structure of these schools is very democratic; children are trusted to complete the assigned work and are allowed to move around freely in and outside the classroom. Children in these schools begin to see themselves as people who make things happen. The bottom line is that children in the affluent-professional and the executive-elite schools are expected to achieve and succeed in life and are taught in ways that empower them to do so.

Finn (2009) argued, and we concur, that although not done intentionally, these differentiated perceptions and treatment of children by teachers are accomplished as part of the hegemonic social order expected in today's unequal society. As studies such as Anyon's (1980) demonstrate, it is a given that when students begin school in such different educational settings, the odds are set for them. "I'd like to hope that a child's expectations are not determined on the day she or he enters kindergarten, but it would be foolish to entertain such hope unless there are some drastic changes made" (Finn, 2009, p. 25).

We strongly believe that such change can only begin to happen when practicing and pre-service teachers critically analyze their own values and the assumptions of others in relation to notions of social class. In this way, they can be empowered with the tools needed to challenge the status quo, helping to reduce social class inequity by encouraging all students to become critical and empowered thinkers and doers.

LEARNING OBJECTIVES

This activity will enable teacher candidates to:

- critique educational assumptions and arrangements by identifying contradictions and inconsistencies among social and educational values and practices;
- determine how issues of social class affect educational equity and success in America's schools, and identify educational practices that minimize those effects; and
- critically question underlying assumptions and ideologies about society and schooling.

PROCEDURE

Preparation[1]

Prior to the day of this activity, instruct students to read chapter 2 in Patrick Finn's (2009) *Literacy with an Attitude: Educating Working-Class Children in Their Own Self-Interest*, where he described Jean Anyon's study. Students should be expected to come to class ready to discuss it and collaborate with their classmates in the creation of two charts. In addition, instructors should either print or have readily available for students the four tables that are listed below (sources for these tables are at the end of the chapter):

- Average After-Tax Income by Income Group. This table shows how income inequalities have widened from 1979 to 2004 from the Center on Budget and Policy Priorities website.

- Share of aggregate income received by each fifth and top 5 percent of households. This table shows data from 1970 to 2009 from the United States Census Bureau website.
- Class in the United States pertaining to personal income and educational attainment for those ages 25 or older by Thompson and Hickey.
- Predictor of SAT performance based on annual family income from the Educational Testing Service website.

Duration: This activity takes 3–4 class hours to complete.
Materials needed: Overhead projector connected to a computer with a word processor or a blackboard.
Steps:

1. At the beginning of the class session, place the Peter McLaren quote provided at the beginning of this chapter on the overhead or board and read it aloud.
2. Read and discuss with the students the above mentioned tables, helping them understand how the continuous gap in social class in America is widening and how the poor are getting poorer and the rich are getting richer.
3. With students, place the schools described in the reading assignment (Finn, 2009) in their respective socio-economic brackets according to both websites (Center on Budget and Policy Priorities and United States Census Bureau website).
4. Create 4 groups of students and assign each group one school described in the reading assignment (working, middle, affluent professional, and executive elite). Instruct students to complete all 6 columns in Chart 1[2] (at the end of this chapter).
5. After each group finishes their portion of the chart, bring together the entire class to complete one whole chart on the overhead or board with all the information provided from each group.
6. Bring out Chart 2, copy and paste all the information provided on Chart 1 columns 4, 5, and 6 onto Chart 2's columns 1, 2, and 3.
7. Complete column 4 on Chart 2 with the entire class (what employment/career are these children being prepared for?). To complete this column, students need to critically analyze and discuss the teaching and learning that is occurring in each of these schools, the kinds of thinkers this type of teaching and learning can create, and the kinds of careers/employments that require this type of thinking.
8. After completing column 4 on Chart 2, return to Chart 1 and revisit column 1 that shows the parent's educational attainment and/or employment. Allow students to read, compare, and contrast it with Chart 2 column 4 that shows the employment/career the children are being prepared for (similar if not the same careers/employ-

ments will be on both parents' and children's career/employment columns).

9. Before completing column 5 on Chart 2, again bring out the Peter McLaren quote provided at the beginning of this chapter, read it and allow students time to read it on their own.

10. Complete column 5 on Chart 2 by discussing with students if the teachers in the Anyon (1980) study are perpetuating or challenging social inequalities.

11. Finish the activity by discussing with students the many ways teachers can challenge these social inequalities in their classrooms. Instructors can also share the Finn (2009) quote from this chapter where he called for "drastic changes" to initiate the discussion.

School	Col. 1	Col. 2	Col. 3	Col. 4	Col. 5	Col. 6
	Parent's educational attainment and/or employment	Annual family income	SAT scores	Teaching methods, teacher expectations, treatment of children, use of textbooks, and how children define knowledge	Authoritarian or democratic setting	Banking or concept/problem solving approach
Working Class						
Middle Class						
Affluent, Professional Class						
Executive, Elite Class						

Chart 1

	Column 1	Column 2	Column 3	Column 4	Column 5
School	Teaching methods, teacher expectations, treatment of children, use of textbooks, and how children define knowledge	Authoritarian or democratic setting	Banking or concept/problem solving approach	What employment or careers are children being prepared for?	Are teachers perpetuating or challenging social inequalities?
Working Class					
Middle Class					
Affluent, Professional Class					
Executive, Elite Class					

Chart 2

SOURCES FOR OTHER TABLES AND CHARTS

Table 1: Average After Tax Income by Income Group (in 2004 dollars). Center of Budget and Policy Priorities http://www.cbpp.org/cms/?fa=view&id=957

Table 694: Share of Aggregate Income Received by Each Fifth and Top 5 Percent of Households: 1970 to 2009. United States Census Bureau http://www.census.gov/compendia/statab/2012/tables/12s0694.pdf

Class in the United States pertaining to personal income and educational attainment for those ages 25 or older by Thompson and Hickey http://en.wikipedia.org/wiki/Social_class_in_the_United_States

Baird, L. (1984). The Correlates of SAT Test Scores and Self Reported Income on the Student Descriptive Questionnaire. New Jersey: Educational Testing Service. http://www.ets.org

REFERENCES

Anyon, J. (1980). Social class and the hidden curriculum of work. *Journal of Education*, 162(1), 67–93.

Finn, P. (2009). *Literacy with an attitude: Educating working-class children in their own self-interest* (2nd ed.). Albany, NY: SUNY Press.

Freire, P. (2000). *Pedagogy of the oppressed* (30th anniversary ed.). New York: Continuum.

McLaren, P. (2003). *Life in schools: An introduction to critical pedagogy in the foundations of education* (4th ed.). Boston: Allyn and Bacon.

NOTES

1. Preceding the introduction of the topic on social class in education, we recommend that students be exposed to readings and critical discussions that cover topics such as Paulo Freire's banking concept and problem-posing types of education, John Dewey's notions of democratic education, and other writings on the effects of authoritarian versus democratic settings on children's social, emotional, and cognitive development.

2. This chart requires that students utilize the tables, charts, and the Finn (2009) reading assignment to provide the following information: Parent's educational attainment and/or employment, annual family income, SAT scores of students based on parent's annual income, teacher expectations and treatment of children, use of textbooks or outside sources, how children define knowledge, if the school setting is democratic or authoritarian; and finally, if the teaching is based on the banking or problem-posing methods of education.

Activity 15

Middle Class Mentality: Using an Online Course Assignment to Teach Students to Know Self First, Then Other

Randall E. Osborne and Paul Kriese

ABSTRACT

When we set out to construct our online course on prejudice, discrimination, and hate, we knew that some variation of a Scholarship of Teaching and Learning (SoTL) pedagogy would be needed (e.g., Hutchings & Shulman, 1999; Osborne, Kriese, Tobey & Johnson, 2009a). We could not expect students to truly grapple with the issues of prejudice, discrimination, and hate, without a critical questioning (Kuhn, 1999) and answering methodology. Otherwise we would, as one of our colleagues put it, "simply teach them how to hate."

The emphasis in this assignment, then, is on self first, then other. In this manner, we believe "other" takes on more meaning because the student is required to always analyze his or her own views and opinions first. Without this analysis, those opinions may "activate" and influence how the student approaches the "other" without any awareness on the part of the student that these biases have been activated.

PURPOSE AND BACKGROUND

The theoretical principle underlying our classroom is Social Identity Theory. Research on (self and) identity suggests that individuals develop a "personal identity"—our sense of our own attributes and a "social identity"—our sense of which groups define who we are (Hogg, 2003). Richard may think of himself as "trustworthy" (a personal identity) and as a "Protestant" (a social identity).

The importance of Social Identity Theory for our course can be found in the implications of social identity for our interactions with and assumptions about other people (e.g., Tajfel & Turner, 1986). Social Identity Theory suggests that people: (a) categorize—it is often useful (indeed, we might be perceived as having the need) to place people and objects into categories, (b) identify—we align ourselves with groups and gain identity and self-esteem from those identifications, and (c) compare—we compare ourselves to others. Those groups with which we identify are called "in-groups," whereas those we compare ourselves (and our "in-groups") to can be considered "out-groups" (e.g., Tajfel & Turner, 1986).

Tajfel and Turner (1986) suggested that we have a tendency to positively define the groups with which we identify so we can more positively evaluate ourselves. This identification results in a self-serving bias. This means if I assign a positive value to "my" groups (in-groups), I am likely to do so by assigning negative value to the groups with which I do not identify (out-groups). If "we" are good, "they" must be bad. In-group becomes the definition of what is "good" so the "other" must be bad.

Additionally, most people rate themselves above average on most dimensions—something social psychologists call the "better-than-most effect." This appears to hold, for example, for fairness (Messick, Bloom, Boldizar, & Samuelson, 1985), happiness (Lykken & Tellegen, 1996), and satisfaction in personal relationships (Buunk & van den Eijnden, 1997). Brown and Kobayashi (2002) suggested that this tendency to assume that we are "better-than-most" extends to members of our social circles so that we believe that members of our families, our friends, and our in-groups are also "better-than-most."

The significant question for our course is how to focus on self as a framework for understanding "other" without initiating social identity theory tendencies to categorize, identify, and compare. Additionally, this goal is further complicated by concerns about the course being taught in an online environment where nonverbal cues are missing (Osborne, Kriese & Tobey, 2008; Osborne, Kriese, Tobey & Johnson, 2009b). This is sometimes referred to in the online teaching and learning literature as the lack of "real world practice" skills that occurs in online teaching environments (e.g., Doo, 2006).

In our classroom, then, the "other" looks like "self." We do not "allow" students to simply search for prejudice, discrimination, and hate by pointing outward and looking at others. We require them to look at "self" over and over and then compare what they are learning about "self" to "others." In order to enhance the likelihood that this self-exploration would result in the kinds of self-knowing that would prepare students to be appropriately positioned to look at "others," however, we knew we needed a well-defined model for self-exploration. We outline this model for students before having them complete any of the course assignments.

LEARNING OBJECTIVES

We expect students to demonstrate a significant amount of critical think-ing in this course. Because this is so important, we have developed, and outlined below, a model that could be used to complete course assign-ments. Specifically, we believe that critical thinkers demonstrate the abil-ity to address issues at each of the following levels:

- Recitation—stating known facts or opinions. A critical component of this step is to acknowledge what aspect(s) of what is being stated is factual and what is based on opinion.
- Exploration—analyzing the roots of those opinions or facts. This step requires digging below the surface of what is believed or known and working to discover the elements that have combined to result in that fact or that opinion.
- Understanding—involves an awareness of other views and a com-prehension of the difference(s) between one's own opinion (and the facts or other opinions upon which that opinion is based) and the opinions of others. To truly "understand" our own opinion in rela-tionship to others, we must initiate an active dialogue with the other person about his or her opinions and the roots of those opin-ions.
- Appreciation—meaning a full awareness of the differences between our views and opinions and those of others. To truly appreciate differences, we must be aware of the nature of those differences. The active dialogue undertaken in the third step (understanding) should lead to an analysis of the opinion as recited by the "other."

In our view, it is important to acknowledge that "understanding" does not mean to "accept." The goal is not to get everyone to agree; the goal is that people will truly explore and understand how and why opinions differ. To understand means to realize the circumstances and motivations that lead to difference and to realize that those differences are meaning-ful.

Discussing social issues such as prejudice or racism, without requiring students to explore the roots of their views, to understand the roots of other views, and to appreciate the nature and importance of different views about those issues, perpetuates ignorance. To raise the issue with-out using the elements of critical thinking and exploration we have out-lined above may simply reinforce prejudices by giving them voice with-out question.

PROCESS

Working together in the chatroom designated for your group, students are instructed that their goals are to:

1. get to know each other, decide on a group name, and use that name in all group posts and in all group assignments.
2. reach consensus on how to define "middle class mentality."
3. post that group definition to the discussion list. In your response, be sure to include answers to the following questions:

   - can anyone "become" middle class? Why or why not?
   - what different aspects of society does the middle class mentality permeate?
   - how is the concept of middle class mentality linked to psychological issues such as social comparison, optimal distinctiveness, and self-perception theory?

Note: students will need to look these three terms up (an Internet search will reveal many resources and most social psychology textbooks cover these). Include a brief discussion of each of these theories into your post, and link your definition to those terms.

SAMPLE STUDENT RESPONSES TO THE ASSIGNMENT

- "Middle Class Mentality can be defined as the baseline to rate oneself on the social scale; it is a frame of mind generally perpetuated by the media, government, and in essence the American Dream. We believe that anyone can become middle class with enough effort. As mentioned previously, the middle class is all in how we perceive it in our mind. For instance, while we would consider ourselves middle class, someone more wealthy may view us as lower class and someone poor as upper class, it's all relative. From a monetary standpoint, it's easy for one's social class to alter.

  If the economy were to downsize forcing companies to close and lay off employees, the wealthy could be demoted to middle class, the middle class to poor, and so on. On the opposite end of the spectrum, if the economy were to increase, it could create new jobs, promotions, or academia advancement."
- "Middle class mentality appears to permeate the point in which to measure yours and others' success and/or failures. It's an ideal that anything can be within your grasp with enough hard work and effort. Our teachers who ask us to try a little bit harder to get that amazing job one day; our boss asking us to put in a little more time for that big promotion; the reality television shows that promise to make you the next big star; essentially it's all around us."

- "Social comparison theory is linked to middle class mentality in that in order to determine our own social standing we are constantly comparing ourselves to those around us and the possessions that the middle-class person does and does not have. The social comparison between the pyramids (poor, middle class, rich), links into the self-perception theory. There are two different social comparisons, upward and downward. Upward would be those comparing themselves to someone of upper status they felt were above them, and downward would be someone who looked upon someone's troublesome time as being worse than theirs."

- "In the self-perception theory we modify our attitudes and feelings based upon observations of ourselves in how we behave in certain situations. The changing of one's attitude can be based upon the social standing of that person and their own feelings about where they would like to be, and where they are at. Our social standings do have an effect in the way one carries oneself and one's attitude.

    The poor might look at every day as a struggle and only wish to be in a higher standard, so their attitude might be perceived as negative, while the wealthy might see their standing in good ratings and view themselves in a positive manner. It differs based upon your own personal goals and beliefs. One might be poor, but have faith that one day they will overcome their struggle, so their viewing of themselves could be positive."

- "Optimal distinctiveness 'asserts that individuals desire to attain an optimal balance of assimilation and distinction within and between social groups and situations (Brewer, 2003).' Optimal distinctiveness is a psychological fight between the two categories. The two are always in constant opposition to each other.

    When there is too much of one motive being drawn out, then the other, the balance of the two becomes thrown off and the other motive must be worked twice as hard to make up for the counterbalance. Middle-class mentality is linked to this idea because middle-class persons usually put more effort into one of the characteristics, which is usually assimilation. It is easy to do something, but it is much harder to add the uniqueness and distinctiveness to counterbalance the other characteristic."

REFERENCES

Brewer, M. B. (2003). Optimal Distinctiveness, Social Identity, and the Self. In M. Leary and J. Tangney (Eds.), *Handbook of Self and Identity*. (pp. 480–491). New York: Guilford.

Brown, J. D., & Kobayashi, C. (2002). Self-enhancement in Japan and America. *Asian Journal of Social Psychology, 5*, 145–67.

Buunk, B. P., & Van den Eijnden, R. J. J. M. (1997). Perceived prevalence, perceived superiority, and relationship satisfaction: Most relationships are good, but ours is better. *Personality and Social Psychology Bulletin, 23*, 219–28.

Doo, Y. M. (2006). A problem in online interpersonal skills training: Do learners practice these skills? *Open Learning, 21*, 263–72.

Hogg, M. A. (2003). Social identity. In M. R. Leary & J. P. Tangney (Eds.), *Handbook of self and identity* (pp. 462–79). New York: Guilford.

Hutchings, P., & Shulman, L. S. (1999). The scholarship of teaching: New elaborations, new developments. *Change, 31*, 10–15.

Kuhn, D. (1999). A developmental model of critical thinking. *Educational Researcher, 28*, 16–26, 46.

Lykken, D., & Tellegen, T. (1996). Happiness is a stochastic phenomenon. *Psychological Science, 7*(3), 186–89.

Messick, D. M., Bloom, S., Boldizar, J. P., & Samuelson, C. D. (1985). Why we are fairer than others. *Journal of Experimental Social Psychology, 21*, 480–500.

Osborne, R. E., Kriese, P., & Tobey, H. (2008). Reflections on a decade of using the scholarship of teaching and learning. *Insight: A Journal of Scholarly Teaching, 3*, 37–46.

Osborne, R. E., Kriese, P., Tobey, H., & Johnson (2009a). Putting it all together: Incorporating "SoTL Practices" for teaching interpersonal and critical thinking skills in an online course. *InSight: A Journal of Scholarly Teaching, 4*, 45–55.

Osborne, R. E., Kriese, P. Tobey. H. & Johnson (2009b). And never the two shall meet?: Student vs. faculty perceptions of online courses. *Journal of Educational Computing Research, 40*, 171–82.

Tajfel, H., & Turner, J. C. (1986). The social identity theory of intergroup behavior. In S. Worchel & W. Austin (Eds.), *Psychology of intergroup relations* (pp. 7–24). Chicago: Nelson-Hall.

Activity 16

Getting to Know You: A Simulation to Understand
School Context

Joanne Caniglia, Ph.D.

ABSTRACT

The nature of this activity is practical and addresses the call for teacher candidates' greater awareness of contextual characteristics of their field placement school and district. The author designed a simulation requiring pre-service teachers to collect data on the school where they will be student teaching, and using the lower quartile salary of the district, attempt to live a month on the salary. Participants often experience cognitive dissonance, as some of their preconceived notions about students and teaching conflict with their vision of what teaching should be like in their district.

BACKGROUND AND PURPOSE

Pre-service teachers hold notions about how students learn based on their own experiences as learners. These experiences can prove an effective starting point for extending their perspectives beyond their own experiences. "Programs that successfully change beginning teachers' understanding about teaching and learning use their students' initial beliefs about teaching as a springboard for surfacing and confronting misconceptions." (Darling-Hammond & Baratz-Snowden, 2007, p. 117). Simulations are an effective means for pre-service teachers to identify and challenge their preconceived notions about their students and their backgrounds.

The purpose of this simulation is to provide meaningful opportunities for participants, especially student teachers, to develop awareness of some of the socioeconomic aspects of the community where they will teach. One method that is useful in sensitizing teachers to issues of poverty and diversity in their student teaching district is a simulation. By using kinesthetic and affective modes of learning, simulations encourage students to analyze and reflect through experiential learning.

Through this simulation, participants attempt to live on the monthly income of a 25-year-old adult from their district. This simulation is an adaptation of the Reality Store®, a program created by Indiana Professional Business Women, addressing educational attainment and financial security. In this adaptation of the Reality Store®, participants are not allowed to choose their occupation; rather, they are given the lower quartile income range for individuals in the school district.

Representatives from the housing industry, utilities, grocery stores, department stores, financial institutions, medical professions, childcare centers, travel and entertainment industry, and so forth participate in the one day event to help future teachers determine how families within their school districts manage with everyday expenses (See figure 16.1). A necessary requirement is reflection on the decisions their students and parents face on a daily basis.

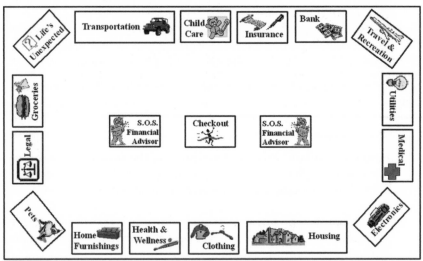

Figure 16.1

LEARNING OBJECTIVES

Goals of the Reality Store® simulation for pre-service teachers include:

- gaining an understanding of the daily routine of individuals and families living in poverty (in their district) and those who live in affluence;

- developing skills to empower future teachers as they work among families who live in poverty; and
- developing a curriculum plan of awareness and action.

PROCEDURE

- Before the Reality Store® visit, students will bring the socioeconomic demographics of the school district in which they will student teach to a methods class for a preliminary discussion. This information will include median income, age, and education.
- Students will follow the 15 stations of the Reality Store® making decisions based upon the demographic information and annual income of residents of their district. For example at the Clothing Station, they will have a choice of purchasing clothes at Macy's, Sears, or WalMart. Each station will have options that require participants to make choices based upon their school districts' median income and demographics. When at the Transportation Station, choices may include bus, cars, bikes, or walking. In addition to making choices, students maintain a check register.
- Upon completing the Reality Store®, participants will complete a written reflection of what choices individuals in their school district are forced to make. Students follow the following format.

Write a "teaching and learning context" statement describing your practicum placement. It is important that you have an introduction and a conclusion to this narrative. You should attempt to address as many of the following criteria as possible:

a) School and district factors: description of the district (rural, urban, middle class, etc.), diversity, percentage on free/reduced lunch, school report card data, relevant data about achievement gap groups.

b) Classroom factors: physical features of the classrooms, availability of technology, extent of parental involvement in the classroom, grouping patterns, scheduling.

c) Student characteristics: ages, gender breakdown, race/ethnicity, special needs, developmental levels, gap-group representations, learning styles, students' skills and prior learning.

d) Implications for instruction: describe two or three ways the above factors impact planning and implementing instruction.

e) Classroom management: in light of your contextual description, describe your expectations for classroom discipline and behavior management, classroom rules, and other processes you observed that promote a classroom environment conducive to student learning.

In light of your observations and the data presented above, describe what you have learned that will impact your practice as a new teacher. Students will conduct an online search from the United States Census and complete table 16.1 (following page), containing relevant demographics.

This listing of demographic characteristics can be found under "State Information" with the option of entering your county or city school district, on the Web at http://quickfacts.census.gov/qfd/states/.

ADDITIONAL COMMENTS

"I never realized what some of the people in my district go through. I drive to my school in areas that are pretty nice and I didn't realize that so many of my students do not live like that."

"Is this real? Why did you insist that we have children?"

"I need a loan . . . but the short term lenders are charging too much interest, but it is the only place I can go."

The comments above, together with ninety-four other students' comments, were collected following a two-hour simulation with future teachers. After completing the simulation, students reflected on four questions: (a) What do you think was the most successful part of this simulation? (b) What was the least successful part of this simulation? (c) Would you recommend this simulation? (d) Any other comments?

Overwhelmingly, students agreed that the simulation helped them to see their school district in a new light. A few thought that it was not "real" and they suggested ways to improve the content of each station. Although each station's content and options were thoroughly researched using U.S. Census data, local school district demographics, and current prices from numerous stores in a one hundred–mile radius of the university, the vast majority of students never realized the many constraints that were placed on families, especially those in poverty.

Given the connection between poverty and education, future teachers (all teachers) will often come in contact with individuals who are living in poverty. To be effective teachers, they must begin to grasp the many dimensions of poverty and the challenges that face those who are poor and who are different than themselves (Cochran-Smith, 2000). Thus, knowledge of their students' context and culture needs to begin at the undergraduate level and with the desire to know their students, despite the fact that future teachers may have limited exposure or personal experience with this population.

The "Getting to Know You" Simulation is a small step toward helping students to not only understand their school districts' context but also to experience the many issues that face those living in poverty (beyond one month!).

a. Sex	Female_____ Male_____
b. Race and Hispanic Origin	White_____ Non-Hispanic _____ Black _____ Asian and Pacific Islander _____ Hispanic (any race) _____
DESIGNATED PARENT	
c. Marital Status	Married _____ Separated, divorced, widowed _____ Never married _____
d. Educational Attainment	Less than high school _____ High school graduate _____ Some college _____ Vocational certificate or associate's degree _____ Bachelor's degree _____ Advanced degree _____
FAMILY	
e. Poverty Status	Below poverty level _____ At or above poverty level _____ 100 to 199 percent of poverty _____ 200 percent of poverty or higher _____
f. Program Participation	Received aid from at least one of the following: TANF _____ Food stamps _____ WIC _____ Medicaid _____ National School Lunch Program _____ Did not receive aid _____
g. Sex	Male _____ Female _____
h. Race and Hispanic Origin	White_____ Non-Hispanic _____ Black _____ Asian and Pacific Islander _____ Hispanic (any race) _____
DESIGNATED PARENT	
i. Marital Status	Married _____ Separated, divorced, widowed _____ Never married _____
j. Educational Attainment	Less than high school _____ High school graduate _____ Some college _____ Vocational certificate or associate's degree _____ Bachelor's degree _____ Advanced degree _____
FAMILY	
k. Poverty Status	Below poverty level _____ At or above poverty level _____ 100 to 199 percent of poverty _____ 200 percent of poverty or higher _____
l. Program Participation	Received aid from at least one of the following: TANF _____ Food stamps _____ WIC_____ Medicaid _____ National School Lunch Program _____ Did not receive aid _____

Table 16.1.

REFERENCES

Business and Professional Women's Clubs of Indiana. (2009). Reality Store®. Knightstown, IA: Author.

Cochran-Smith, M. (2000). Blind vision: Unlearning racism in teacher education. *Harvard Educational Review, 70*, 157–90.

Darling-Hammond, L., & Baratz-Snowden, J. (Eds.). (2007, Winter). A good teacher in every classroom: Preparing the highly qualified teachers our children deserve. *Educational Horizons*, 111–32.

Dye, J. L., & Johnson, T. D. (2009). A child's day: 2006 (Selected Indicators of Child Well- Being). Current Population Reports, P70-118. U.S. Census Bureau, Washington, DC.

Activity 17

Person Like Me

Jason C. Fitzgerald and April A. Mattix

Only by knowing and understanding each other's experiences can we find common ground on which we can examine and resolve our differences.

—President Jimmy Carter, 1977

ABSTRACT

An increasingly diverse country necessitates a careful consideration of how we prepare new and pre-service teachers to develop their cultural awareness and competencies. The following lesson provides teachers with a tangible experience of seeing the world through a sociocultural perspective unlike their own and exploring the ways in which power and privilege impact lives. The lesson enables individuals to experience the rich and diverse backgrounds and experiences that students bring with them to the classroom, especially those that are dissimilar from their own.

BACKGROUND AND PURPOSE

The students comprising K–12 classes across the United States today look very different from those of only a decade ago. The number of new immigrants has increased (Camarota, 2012), while minority populations are spreading more evenly across the nation (Institute of Education Sciences: National Center for Education Statistics, n.d.). While this shift necessitates that we attend carefully to incorporating culturally relevant pedagogies, it also provides the opportunity to focus on efforts to enrich classroom discussions about power, privilege, equity, difference, and social justice.

As teacher educators, our challenge is to enable all pre-service teachers to connect with students who have differing life experiences and analyze the systemic effects that difference has on how we approach the vast multitude of learners who enter the classroom. Our goal is to stimulate curiosity about the world, provide opportunities for developing cultural self-confidence, build awareness and respect for human dignity and diversity, and encourage the exploration of human universals.

The following activity is situated in sociocultural theory, which posits that societies impact an individual's development (Vygotsky, 1934/1986); pre-service teachers' life experiences have explicitly and implicitly shaped their perspectives about the world. These experiences differ from those of their students, regardless of shared social characteristics. To engage their students in meaningful learning, teachers need to be familiar with the impact those differences have on power and privilege in the classroom and become comfortable with engaging "difference" as an asset rather than a challenge.

Before pre-service teachers can design effective lessons and create appropriate environments to illustrate and foster "difference as asset," they must first develop it for themselves, working with and reflecting upon the roles social characteristics play in their own lives and the lives of people with whom they are not altogether familiar or comfortable. Through doing so, pre-service teachers have the opportunity to help develop the skills and attitudes necessary to create empowering classroom cultures and help students engage in meaningful dialog on complex social situations.

To be sure, this is a deeply personal and highly individualized task. It first requires pre-service teachers to reflect upon their own lives, honestly evaluating their own experiences in terms of the system of privilege in which they operate. Second, it requires them to risk working with "an other," moving out of their comfort zone to engage a person who is different. Third, it requires pre-service teachers to analyze the ways in which the system of privilege has impacted the life of that other individual, examining the individual choices that the person made through a lens of privilege.

Throughout all of these steps, pre-service teachers must reflect, making connections between what they are learning about themselves, others, and the system of privilege that informs their understanding of how to teach for a more socially just world. While no one classroom activity can encompass the meaningful experiences that pre-service teachers need to provide in a multicultural world, in our experience, one activity has successfully begun these conversations, enabling pre-service teachers to begin their examination of broader society: the Person Like Me experience.

The Person Like Me activity can be used at almost any point in a class where pre-service teachers are required to visit "diverse" sites, as described below, and interview people who are different from themselves based on social characteristics. The aim of this activity is to reduce epistemic closure, a learned behavior where individuals associate with and listen to people who look like and have similar views to themselves, not to just meet different people. Reflection and dialog play a critical role in this activity, pushing pre-service teachers to evaluate their findings through the lens of power and privilege.

LEARNING OBJECTIVES

Throughout the course of the activity, there are three primary learning objectives. Participants will (1) demonstrate an awareness of and sensitivity to individuals from diverse backgrounds, (2) analyze and evaluate power relationships and social inequality based on the social characteristics of gender/sexual orientation, race/ethnicity, and class; and (3) create paradigms of cultural diversity to guide the development and implementation of learning and teaching strategies.

PROCEDURE

The Person Like Me activity has four procedural elements; however, there is some preparation that needs to be done prior to the start of the activity. Before the students select a place where they might be "an other," they must understand that this assignment is not a means to make anyone feel guilty about their own privilege. It is also not an attack on their own morals, values, and/or beliefs, or a search for an individual from whom we can make generalizations about the whole. Instead, this is an activity to learn more about the students they will teach.

Since pre-service teachers bring deeply personal values to issues of diversity, this activity is not one that should be conducted at the very beginning of any course. Rather, helping students to understand that (a) we are responsible for power and privilege but not responsible for the past, (b) we are charged with learning about and with all students regardless of our own moral convictions, and (c) individuals can expand our own insight but not serve as generalized data can all take a couple of weeks. These realizations could take students some time to internalize and thus make this activity more meaningful.

A resource that has proven very useful over the years to help students engage in these discussions is Allan Johnson's (2006) book *Privilege, Power, and Difference*. His argument provides a theoretical platform that many students find nonconfrontational and from which they can reorient themselves to others who are not "like them." Beginning these discussions in the theoretical, rather than beginning in individuals' experiences, enables students to remove their own feelings from the sociological realities of "difference," and thus provides for more productive conversations.

Step 1: Find a person by visiting a "diverse" site.

After classroom dialogs that reduce pre-service teachers' possible anxieties about confronting power and privilege disparities in a system from which many of them have benefited, students must select a site where they might find "an other." Since this activity is both a self-exploratory and sociological exercise, it is important for students to select a site that they think might help them push into new worlds that they seldom or never frequent. It is there that they will find the people whom they might most need to interview. Table 17.1 provides some possible diversity sites that we have given our students.

When we distribute this list, we note three important considerations for our students' site selections: (1) choose a site with which you are unfamiliar and think might provide information that will help you in your career working with diverse students; (2) if you do not feel ready to see "an other" as "like you," do not select that as a site right now; and (3) only do what feels safe, preferably going to any of these sites with a partner. It is vital that students both push themselves to experience meaningful interactions *and* stay safe. If either qualification is not met, the activity loses its purpose.

Category	Possible Experiences
Social class	Attend a soup kitchen, standing in line and eating with those at the kitchen Visit a social security office Visit a homeless shelter
Religion	Attend a service not of your predominant faith Visit a center of worship and participate in a religious studies class (e.g., Sunday School)
Gender/Sexuality	Volunteer at a rape crisis center or battered women's center Visit a gay bar (students age 21 and older)
Race/Ethnicity	Visit a minority house of worship Shop in an ethnic neighborhood Take part in an ethnic pride day event
Language	Attend a worship service not in your own language
Exceptionality	Volunteer at a program for adults with disabilities Volunteer with the Leukemia and Lymphoma Society Visit and/or volunteer at a Special Olympics event

Table 17.1.

Step 2: Conduct a personal interview.

When students visit a site, we remind them that their primary goal is not to provide services at the sites, although many choose to do so when their responsibilities for this assignment have been completed. Rather, students should get to know people. They should focus on learning their life stories, trying to empathize with their situations and, most importantly, seeing the person as a person like him- or herself, but with a different life trajectory and perspective.

A common concern among students is that they feel awkward initiating conversations with strangers, especially in unfamiliar contexts. Over the years, the students who have had the most success have been honest about this discomfort and have slowly entered into the unfamiliar environments. Often, they arrive at the site and wait a few moments before approaching anyone, exploring the atmosphere and rhythm of the place while acclimating themselves.

When students ask someone near them if they can chat, they explain that they are preparing to be teachers and want to better understand the society in which they will teach. Most people want to help out students and are excited to share their stories. Asking probing questions like, "What led to that happening?" and "What do you think could have been done to change your circumstances?" helps them understand that person's unique story and life experience and exposes the individual's story and some of the more systemic issues of power and privilege that result in vastly different perspectives.

Perhaps the most exciting part of this experience is that many of the individuals who chat with students also take the role as teacher, asking students about their own lives and how they have accomplished all that they have. These interviews often develop into two-way conversations, providing students a chance to learn of another's story while also exploring how the system of power and privilege has impacted their own lives in a way and setting that is more authentic than in the classroom. These interactions enable richer reflections and deeper understandings of the systemic role of power and privilege.

Step 3: Write a reflection.

The written reflection component of this activity should be completed in at least two sittings. First, students should immediately write down the interviewee's story, highlighting their first impressions of how that person's life has been influenced by the situations in which they found themselves. After a couple of days, students should revisit those thoughts and connect the story to class discussions and readings as well as to their own lives.

In the end, the reflection should include a brief narrative of the interviewee's life, how their life has been impacted by their unique experiences, how those connections relate to the literature, and how that person is like the student. We ask students to complete these reflections in two parts, as it often takes time for students to look beyond those personal pieces and make connections to broader theoretical frames. Writing the reflection in two parts helps students digest what they have heard, both in class and at the site.

Step 4: Dialog and make connections.

After students write their reflections, it is time to bring those experiences back together as a class. Although it is tempting to let students lead these discussions, we have found that some students fear sharing personal insights with the class. For example, one student who analyzed his hostility towards homosexuals after visiting a gay bar never did feel comfortable sharing his changing feelings with the class. Instead, by pre-reading the reflections, the teacher can extract general themes from across the writings, enabling the class to make connections to the theoretical framework.

When students see that theirs was not the only experience that dealt with a particular way privilege is used for power, they can begin to explore how the stories are similar and bring examples to the theory. In this way, students who want to share their personal experiences with the class are able to do so while everyone is able to discuss these themes in general. Otherwise, students can talk about the themes rather than their own experiences, protecting themselves as they continue to analyze and come to terms with their own privilege.

These conversations are also a good time for students to explore non-examples, times when individuals' choices were a leading influence in the interviewees' lives. By pooling themes from across students' experiences, it is possible to dialog about the validity of the theory while recognizing that individual choice plays a role in specific situations. These discussions can then be turned toward how teachers can and should see both individual action and systemic structures as influences in students' lives, opening discussions about how to manage both.

ADDITIONAL COMMENTS

While the Person Like Me activity has defined learning objectives, it can be repeated at intervals throughout the course or during a series of courses, and it can also be used to support other projects, such as policy analyses, digital history projects, and comparative sociology projects. The major impetus to pursuing such activities with our students is our desire to provide opportunities for pre-service teachers to develop an increased awareness of the lives of others.

Lessons, such as the one described here, provide opportunities for pre-service teachers to develop their understanding of culturally responsive curricula and increase their appreciation for the range of diverse learners that populate today's classrooms. Such activities encourage practices that underlie and facilitate the bridging of social and cultural diversity, as well as developing understanding across cultural and social differences, enabling pre-service teachers to make connections with a wide variety of students.

SUGGESTED FURTHER READING

Allen, B. J. (2012). *Difference matters, communicating social identity*. Long Grove, IL: Waveland Press.

Johnson, A. G. (2006). *Privilege, Power, and Difference* (2nd ed.). New York: McGraw-Hill.

Kimmel, M. S., & Ferber, A. L. (2010). *Privilege, a Reader* (2nd ed.). Boulder, CO: West-view Press.

Maurianna, A., Warren, B., Carmelita, C., Heather, H., Madeline, P., & Ximena, Z. (2010). *Readings for Diversity and Social Justice* (2nd ed.). New York: Routledge.

Wiggan, G. (2011). *Power, Privilege and Education: Pedagogy, Curriculum and Student Outcomes*. Hauppauge, NY: Nova Science Publishers.

REFERENCES

Camarota, S. A. (2012, August). Center for immigration studies. Retrieved from http://cis.org/2012-profile-of-americas-foreign-born-population.

Institute of Education Sciences: National Center for Education Statistics. (n.d.). English Language Learners in public schools. Retrieved from http://nces.ed.gov/programs/coe/indicator_ell.asp.

Johnson, A. G. (2006). *Privilege, power, and difference* (2nd ed.). New York: McGraw-Hill.

Vygotsky, L. (1934/1986). *Thought and Language*. Cambridge, MA: The MIT Press.

Activity 18

Crossings, Bridges and Borderlands: An Experiential
Assignment for Multicultural Education

Sofia A. Villenas

ABSTRACT

This assignment is designed for students enrolled in university courses on the subject of multicultural education. It requires students to pursue an event or activity that helps them experience the borders of power, privilege, culture, and difference. This activity involves entering campus or community spaces, and engaging with people who share different political, cultural, ethnic, linguistic, or religious differences or views. Pre-plan and follow-up reflective exercises help guide both the experience and the self-directed learning outcomes.

BACKGROUND AND PURPOSE

Our schools are increasingly multicultural and multiracial. Yet students who enter our university classrooms are coming from ever more segregated neighborhoods and high schools since the *Brown v. Board of Education* decision in 1954 ended de-jure segregation (Orfield, Kucsera, Siegel-Hawley, 2012). Students also come to our university classrooms with taken-for-granted knowledge about a world that is deeply divided by race, class, gender, sexuality, and citizenship status, among other hierarchies. They have experienced and seen the racial and class divides in their tracked honors and "regular" public high school classrooms.

Many students have experienced western-centric and heteronormative curriculum. They see demeaning media representations of women, people of color, Muslims and other non-Christians, queer-identified people (LGBTQ), and people in poverty. They see how lines are strictly drawn between political parties and liberal and conservative "cultures."

These lessons often leave students with a sense of boundaries and borders they feel they cannot cross, and people with whom they feel they cannot empathize.

This activity draws from notions of crossings and "borderlands" (Anzaldúa, 1987). Crossings refer to the lived experiences of people who cross between constructed borders and boundaries of geographies and identities. Many students inhabit those in-between spaces where nations, genders, races, ethnicities, and sexualities collide. Such borderland spaces may be unsettling and tumultuous but also transformative in their educational potential.

This activity invites students to engage in crossings and to experience and cultivate borderlands sensibilities when they enter spaces of difference. How might they build bridges to cross that invite others to cross? How might they build bridges of understanding that lead inward and outward? In this activity, students are asked to engage others in unfamiliar contexts and communities in order to reflect on the difficulties and the promise of learning across difference. This activity is important for prospective teachers' self-reflexive work as they go out to teach in increasingly diverse classrooms.

LEARNING OBJECTIVES

This activity asks students to go to the other side of the fence, to engage "other" people in unfamiliar contexts and communities. It asks students to immerse themselves in the voices and feelings of difference and to pay attention to power, privilege, and culture and to the ensuing emotions. It asks students to stretch and resist the temptation to seek comfortableness, and to reflect on what happens when they are unmoored from their usual locations as they attempt to learn about other people's experiences.

Participants will:

- reflect on their own beliefs and personal experiences with difference;
- explore and identify how histories and society structure their encounter;
- examine how power, privilege, borders, and barriers are working in the encounter;
- identify how their feelings and emotions before, during, and after the event are informed by their previous life experiences and learning; and
- collaborate with other students to identify what they learned about themselves and others (families, communities, cultural groups) and how this may be translated to teaching in diverse classrooms.

PROCESS

- Students read a portion of Gloria Anzaldúa's (1987) *Borderlands/La Frontera* that describes the borderlands. They should also read the preface and some stories from *This Bridge We Call Home: Radical Visions for Transformation*, edited by Gloria Anzaldúa and Analouise Keating (2002). These readings help students think about the everydayness of crossings, bridging, and living life on the metaphorical and geographical borderlands. How do students relate to these stories? The instructor should be careful and nuanced when inviting students to explore how they "cross" and inhabit different borderlands, while pointing out the political nature of crossings, bridges, and borderlands. Disparities of race, gender, class, and citizenship, among other fault lines of injustice, are at the root of the stories in *This Bridge We Call Home*.
- At the beginning of the semester, have each student submit a two-page plan that briefly outlines the following: (a) the groups of people and organizations with which they have been involved on campus; (b) a reflection on which spaces they have not entered or have avoided and/or groups of people with whom they have *not* interacted; and finally (c) a plan that involves interactions with one specific group which they have a genuine interest in learning more about. This choice of group may be based on differences of religion, sexuality, race, ethnicity, politics, or language.

  Students should identify two or three opportunities on campus or in the local community for this engagement, and include specific names of campus organizations and events or community sites. There should be flexibility for attending new events or for opportunities likely to arise in the course of the semester.
- Do advise students that they will need to be very respectful and enter "other" spaces with humility. They might want to accompany a friend who belongs to the particular community or organization, or take a friend along. They will most likely be surprised with the process. Some students will experience it as positive, while others will describe their experiences as negative. It is important to point out that each is a powerful learning experience and can inform future action and change.
- Students will attend their events. They should be allowed to share their experiences informally in class in the weeks that follow and to ask questions.
- On a pre-determined due date, students will come to class with a seven-page reflective essay that describes the events or activities and how they experienced them and that responds to the following questions:

   a. What ideas did you have about the specific group of people? What expectations did you have about the event or interaction?

   b. How did you feel before, during, and after the experiences? What was difficult? Easy? Did your emotions and feelings change over time, and if so, how?

   c. What did you notice and learn about the process of entering another space not your own? How might you have done things differently?

   d. What did you notice and learn about the community of people?

   e. Take it one step further and relate the experience to our discussions and readings about difference in terms of power, privilege, borders, and barriers. Also think about the history, ideologies, beliefs, and/or stereotypes at play at the very moment of your encounter with difference.

- On the same day that students bring in their write-ups, have students discuss the questions below in groups of four students. Students should take turns sharing their responses, making sure that each student has an opportunity to answer each question in go-around fashion. One should facilitate and keep track of time, while another should record the responses. Each small group should report back to the larger group.

   a. What are similarities across your experiences and what are differences?

   b. What did the experience teach you about the process of engaging difference?

   c. In light of your collective experiences, brainstorm a list of words or adjectives that give meaning to "crossings," "bridging" and "borderlands."

   d. How can you translate this process of learning to opportunities for reflection and growth as prospective teachers, or for taking action in your life?

- It is important to debrief students on their experiences as some might have felt them to be negative and, in the process, implicate a particular group of people represented in the class. What is involved (histories, stereotypes, beliefs) when students experience exclusion or unwelcoming glances as they enter a space not their own?

- Students are invited to brainstorm how to represent their learning as a collective, keeping in mind that it might not be appropriate to share particular information that might disrespect a person or groups of people. For example, they may create an e-book that highlights different aspects of their collective learning. They may also share this collective representation with university administration.

REFERENCES

Anzaldúa, G. (1987). *Borderlands/la Frontera: The New Mestiza*. San Fancisco: Aunt Lute Books.

Anzaldúa, G. & Keating, A. (2002). *This Bridge We Call Home: Radical Visions for Transformation*. New York: Routledge.

Orfield, G., Kucsera, J., & Siegel-Hawley, G. (2012). *E pluribus . . . separation: Deepening double segregation for more students*. The Civil Rights Project/*Proyecto Derechos Civiles*, University of California, Los Angeles.

Activity 19

Follow the Multicolored Brick Road to Cultural Competence

Nancy P. Gallavan

ABSTRACT

The Journey to Cultural Competence features eight stages along the path constructed on the Fibonacci Sequence. At each stage, travelers' discoveries inform and support their insights encountered with the other stages as they explore issues of equity and social justice to better understand themselves, one another, and society. En route, educators discover that cultural competence is an ongoing transformational journey accentuated by unforeseen encounters reflected upon as defining moments.

Classroom teachers and teacher educators benefit from insights for infusing the possibilities and parameters associated with cultural competence with their learners; school leaders become valuable conduits for establishing and reinforcing the responsibility for cultural competence within the profession. Professional developers glean guidance for supporting and advancing the levels of cultural competence with classroom teachers, and all educators grow exponentially by reexamining their own cultural competence recursively for modeling and ensuring the presence and power of cultural competence as process and product.

PURPOSE AND BACKGROUND

In the 1939 movie *The Wizard of Oz*, Dorothy and her little dog, Toto, begin their journey by following a yellow brick road that winds around on itself and expands as it curves. This road is built on a mathematical pattern, called the Fibonacci Sequence, as a Fibonacci Spiral. The Fibonacci Sequence is a series of numbers where each new number is the sum of the previous two numbers, for example, 1, 1, 2, 3, 5, 8 . . . continuing indefinitely. When the numbers are used to construct squares (see figure 19.1) and a line is drawn to connect opposing corners, a Fibonacci Spiral is formed. Also known as a "golden spiral," this configuration is found throughout nature in flora (e.g., sunflowers and pinecones), fauna (e.g., nautilus seashells and rams' horns), food (e.g., pineapples and artichokes), the world (e.g., ocean waves and the galaxy), and humans (e.g., fingerprints and ears).

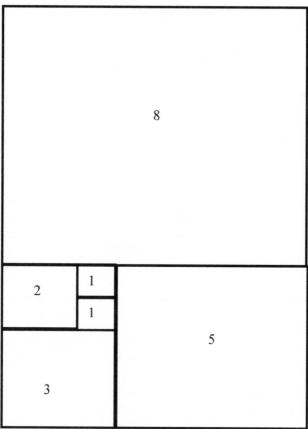

Figure 19.1.

The Fibonacci Spiral paves the path of the Gallavan Journey to Cultural Competence Model (see figure 19.2) highlighted by eight stages of development, the multicolored bricks, detailed in this enlightening teaching and learning strategy (Gallavan & Webster-Smith, 2012). Through the journey, one gains valuable insights about self, others, and society. The journey is highlighted with awareness or *conscientization*; self-assessment manifested as reactions, responses, reciprocity, and reflections; self-efficacy; agency; and critical consciousness, contributing to understanding and practicing equity and social justice.

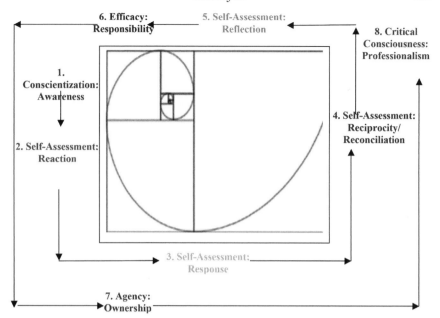

Figure 19.2.

En route, educators discover that cultural competence is an ongoing transformational journey accentuated with unforeseen encounters one reflects upon as defining moments. Classroom teachers and teacher educators benefit from insights for infusing the possibilities and parameters associated with cultural competence with their learners, while school leaders become valuable conduits for establishing and reinforcing the responsibility for cultural competence within the profession. Professional developers glean guidance for supporting and advancing the levels of cultural competence with classroom teachers, and all educators grow exponentially by reexamining their own cultural competence recursively for modeling and ensuring the presence and power of cultural competence as process and product.

GALLAVAN JOURNEY TO CULTURAL COMPETENCE MODEL

Traveling the path to cultural competence encompasses eight stages along the path that everyone experiences through chance and choice. The first stage of the journey awakens perceptions and initiates *conscientization,* or awareness of the basic elements composed of the knowledge, skills, dispositions, and contexts of education. Conscientization describes the processes of increasing an educator's awareness of the world, the variables that impact all aspects of the educator's life, and the capacity to change the world through one's action (Freire, 1970).

Freire tells us that conscientization develops through four broadening levels of maturation beginning with intransitive consciousness (preoccupation with basic needs and limited or no comprehension of one's sociocultural situation), moving through the levels of semi-intransitivity or magical consciousness (presumption that one's sociocultural situation is predestined and should be accepted for all time), advancing to semi-transitive consciousness, or popular consciousness (initiation of control over one's life through more conversations and wider circle of exposure and influence), and ultimately realizing critical consciousness (thoughtful inquiries and meaningful interpretations displayed through self-confidence, risk taking, actions, and responsibility).

The next four stages of the journey help educators map the four components of self-assessment by acknowledging and analyzing one's existence in terms of one's cultural capital (background, beliefs, behaviors, similarities, differences, dispositions, habits, power, privileges, advantages, opportunities, disadvantages, and barriers) in multiple contexts. The four stages include reaction, response, reciprocity, and reflection.

Reactions tend to be presented as quick retorts that may or may not be expressed with much thought or consideration and are frequently generated automatically, emotionally, and noisily. Think of questions that start with the word "what" that elicit unrefined descriptions. For example, every day teachers receive many new requests from their school administrators and students' families. A teacher's typical reaction might be to snap, "What do I have to do now?!?"

Responses tend to be provided as perfunctory replies delivered with some attention and deliberation. By questioners using softer, conversational tones, responses to them are prepared, and obligatory answers are based on knowledge and sources. Think of questions that start with the word "how" that are answered with useful information. For example, when teachers receive requests from their school administrators or students' families, the response could be phrased, "How can I fulfill that request to save the most time?"

Reciprocity tends to be pursued as a quest associated with curious inquiries and substantiated reason eliciting novelty and necessity. Expressed with excitement and hope, reciprocity stimulates new discoveries and possible connections empowering educators to collaborate and exchange ideas. Think of questions that start with the words "what if" that explore plans and possibilities. For example, after receiving a request, the teacher seeks a colleague to check the approaches that the colleague used to complete the task and proposes, "What if I talk with the administrator before I submit my report?"

Reflections tend to be produced as a delayed insight accompanied by mindfulness and contemplation based on relevant significance and holistic objectivity (Schön, 1983). Reflections inspire educators to consider events from the vantage point of teaching, learning, and schooling within the entire educational enterprise. Think of questions that start with the word "why" that examine multiple perspectives. For example, in thinking about the situation related to the request, the teacher contemplates, "I wonder why the administrator tends to make requests after lunch when there is no time for me to stop and fulfill them during the afternoon?"

The sixth stage prompts educators to enhance their self-efficacy (Bandura, 1997) and responsibilities relating to the individual educator's belief in his or her abilities to achieve a goal in the context of teaching and learning. Examining the attributes of self-efficacy emphasizes that the educators' self-perceptions strongly influence the ways actions will be interpreted as successes or failures and influence future thoughts and actions, acknowledging innate, intuitional leadership.

The seventh stage encourages educators to enrich their sense of agency (Bandura, 1989) or ownership for professional teaching, learning, and schooling. Agency extends from critical reflection on one's expertise and experiences prompting an educator to act upon his or her newly evolved understanding of self, others, and society.

The eighth and final stage encompasses the recursive role of educators' critical consciousness as the unifying embodiment of cognizance leading the educational enterprise. Through the journey, the traveler develops perception, preparation, proficiency, professionalism, and purposefulness. The advancing developments create a spiral following the Fibonacci Sequence of numbers enveloping one stage into the next stage with each development increasing the traveler's momentum.

LEARNING OBJECTIVES OF GALLAVAN'S JOURNEY TO CULTURAL COMPETENCE LEARNING EXPERIENCE

The purposes of this learning experience are to prompt the traveler to:

- deconstruct, plan, and analyze awareness and self-assessment, that is, *I do, you watch*;
- examine the critical components of self-efficacy, that is, *I do, you help*;
- probe continuity and intervals in agency, that is, *You do, I help*; and
- connect philosophies with the cultural competence, that is, *You do, I watch*.

To fulfill these purposes, the objective of this learning experience is to guide the traveler along the journey to cultural competence in ways that are honest, natural, authentic, and holistic. Experiences that are honest allow the traveler to increase a sense of trust in self, others, and society. To be natural, experiences must connect with the traveler. To be authentic, experiences must be honored by the traveler as genuine and valid.

Experiences that are holistic must draw from cognitive, affective, physical, and social elements.

PROCEDURE AND DEFINING MOMENTS

The procedures begin with a brief writing assignment. Each traveler is given a sheet of white unlined 8.5" x 11" paper and is asked to turn the paper horizontally.

Step 1: In the upper left-hand corner, each traveler is asked to write this statement and fill in the blanks with an assumption, value, or belief that has influenced the traveler: All _____ are _____. Here is an example statement to share with the travelers: All tall men are good basketball players. In the upper right-hand corner, ask travelers to contextualize the background associated with their statement. Prompt the travelers to extend the context through descriptors addressing who, what, where, how, when, and why. For example, I know a man who is an extraordinarily tall man who did not play basketball.

Step 2: In the lower left-hand corner, ask travelers to remember a time that the traveler or someone related to the situation wished they had intervened but chose not to get involved. For example, a man is a stockbroker. However, in almost every type of situation, people ask him if he played basketball with no regard to his professional career, his personal interests, or his physical abilities. Usually the question is followed with inquiries seeking the reason he did not play basketball and what his height is. The man politely answers that he wasn't interested in playing basketball and that he is 6 foot 9 inches tall.

Step 3: In the lower right-hand corner, ask travelers to remember a time that the traveler or someone related to the situation intervened. The intervention may have been positive and productive or negative and confrontational. For example, my friend shared with me that one time when his son was twelve years old and was with his father, the basketball question was posed, and the son reacted by telling the inquirer that his father is a stockbroker and plays chess.

Step 4: Allow time for travelers to think and write. Then place travelers in groups of no more than four to share their notes. Remind all travelers that no information has to be shared if the traveler feels it is too personal and that all travelers should respect all other travelers' comments and not repeat shared information.

The information shared in this learning experience constitutes some of our Defining Moments (Kidd, Sánchez, & Thorp, 2008). The statements, contexts, absence of intervention, and times of intervention summarize a set of memories that resonate throughout the traveler's life and influence their thoughts, beliefs, words, actions, and interactions (Hyland & Knoffke, 2005). Defining moments leave strong impressions; yet rarely are these moments made visible or shared aloud with other people for validation and understanding.

Step 5: Critical Consciousness. Travelers are given a copy of the Gallavan Journey to Cultural Competence Model (see figure 19.2). Focusing on each of the eight stages one at a time, travelers are asked for their descriptions. After brief conversations, each of the eight stages is explained and connected in the never-ending flow leading to cultural competence. In deconstructing the statements and conversations from Defining Moments, travelers are asked to write the traveler's individual insights and intentions next to each of the eight stages to guide their students.

For example, these notes continue unfolding the events of my friend with the tall father who was always asked if he played basketball.

1. Awareness or *conscientization*: all people have various physical conditions; physical characteristics are part of a person; they do not consume a person's existence or limit a person's possibilities.
2. Self-awareness; reaction: avoid staring at people with physical characteristics that you have not seen or experienced.
3. Self-awareness; response: ask people questions about them as people; do not ask questions based exclusively on a physical characteristic.
4. Self-awareness; reciprocity: ask people if they need assistance if the situation seems appropriate.
5. Self-awareness; reflection: think about times when people have stared or offered assistance when it was not appropriate; think about times when people offered assistance and it was appropriate and appreciated.
6. Self-efficacy: integrate guidelines into the teaching and learning as part of the curricular expectations as well as part of the social interactions emphasizing the value and reward for taking responsibility for one's behaviors.
7. Agency: teach and model the importance of taking ownership for one's thoughts, beliefs, words, actions, and interactions at all times and with all people.
8. Critical consciousness: connect current behaviors with professional goals and standards.

ADDITIONAL COMMENTS

The Journey to Cultural Competence relates to educators in every capacity guiding young learners and to teacher candidates, faculty, staff, colleagues, and community citizens, with reflective practices (DeMulder & Rigsby, 2003). Once the path has been traveled with deliberation, travelers begin to transform as they relate the stages of the journey to new encounters and discoveries (Gay, 2003; Olsen, 2008). As Glenda the Good

Witch urged Dorothy and Toto in *The Wizard of Oz* to follow the yellow brick road, travelers on the journey to cultural competence are encouraged to follow the multicolored brick road.

REFERENCES

Bandura, A. (1989). Human agency in social cognitive theory. *American Psychologist, 44*(9), 1175–84.

Bandura, A. (1997). *Self-Efficacy: The Exercise of Control.* New York: W. H. Freeman.

DeMulder, E. K., & Rigsby, L. C. (2003). Teachers' voices on reflective practice. *Reflective Practice, 4*(3), 267–90.

Freire, P. (1970). *Pedagogy of the Oppressed.* New York: Continuum.

Gallavan, N. P., & Webster-Smith, A. (2012). Cultural competence and the recursive nature of conscientization. In N. P. Gallavan & C. E. Craig (Eds.), *Issues in education; Part I.* ATE Yearbook XXI (pp. 401–19). Philadelphia: Taylor & Francis.

Gay, G. (2003). *Becoming Multicultural Educators: A Personal Journey toward Professional Agency.* San Francisco: Jossey-Bass.

Hyland, N. E., & Knoffke, S. E. (2005). Understanding diversity through social and community inquiry: An action research study. *Journal of Teacher Education, 56*(4), 367–81.

Kidd, J. K., Sánchez, S. Y., & Thorp, E. K. (2008). Defining moments: Developing culturally responsive dispositions and teaching practices in early childhood preservice teachers. *Teaching and Teacher Education, 24*(2), 316–29.

Olsen, B. (2008). *Teaching What They Learn, Learning What They Live: How Teachers' Personal Histories Shape Their Professional Development.* Boulder, CO: Paradigm.

Schön, D. A. (1983). *The Reflective Practitioner: How Professionals Think in Action.* New York: Basic Books.

Activity 20

What Is My Cultural Identity?

Debra L. Clark

ABSTRACT

To move away from ethnocentrism and toward ethnorelativism (see Bennet, 1993) pre-service teachers must first recognize that they are themselves cultural beings. Banks (1998) posits that there are five dimensions to multiculturalism in schools: content integration, knowledge construction, equity pedagogy and prejudice reduction, and empowering school culture and social structure. Teachers cannot work toward these goals if they believe they are the "norm" and if they believe those who are different strive to be like the "norm" they represent.

PURPOSE AND BACKGROUND

Knefelkamp (2003) argues that good teaching and learning can occur only when we understand the positions of our students; the "emphasis on standpoint—the perspectives acquired from one's lived life" (p.10). This is the foundation of social identity theory—the "ability to take into account the influences of gender, race, ethnicity, and socioeconomic class . . . literally one's stance with respect to knowing, making meaning, and making commitments." (p. 11).

One's self-concept is defined by comparing one's own group to that of others (Tajfel & Turner, 1986; Shinnar, 2008). One's group may be the result of a certain ethnicity, gender, or religion, or it could be due to membership in an organization such as the Boy Scouts of America (Banks, 2012). According to Shinnar (2008) if someone has a positive self-concept, it is because they find more merit in the groups to which they belong than the groups from which they are different. This allows an individual to feel a sense of belonging as well as a sense of uniqueness (Padilla & Perez, 2003; Shinnar, 2008).

For teachers of future teachers, however, understanding the positions of students is simply not enough. We must shape our students to become border crossers. According to Coleman (2012), border crossers have the desire and the passion to move beyond the comfort zones of their pre-scribed culture and roles. This skill is what is necessary for our students to effectively teach their increasingly diverse students.

In other words, we must understand the positions of our students and motivate and educate them to become border crossers, while at the same time striving to maintain their self-concepts. We must help students learn that they are simultaneously an individual as well as part of a group, that each has similarities and differences simultaneously, and that they are not completely the same or completely different from each other, their professors, or their future students (Knefelkamp, 1999).

Cushner, McClelland, and Safford (2012) identified twenty-four vari-ables in their Cultural Learning Process, which assist professors and their students in understanding the dynamics of cultural identity—twelve cul-tural identifiers and twelve socialization agents. For the purpose of this discussion, I have condensed these variables into seven cultural identifi-ers and seven socialization agents. Cultural identifiers are variables by which others recognize us and we define ourselves (Cushner, McClel-land, & Safford, 2012; Clark, 2013).

The following are examples of cultural identifiers:

- Ancestry—consisting of ethnicity, nationality, and for some, relig-ious heritage
- Ability—consisting of cognitive, physical, and emotional abilities and disabilities
- Location—consisting of type (rural, suburban, or urban), region, citizenship, and global membership
- Social class and status—consisting of the privileges or suppressions one is afforded due to income and associated respect or lack of respect one receives despite one's income
- Gender—male, female, transgendered
- Age—peer cohort and chronological age
- Language—written and verbal, dialect, nonverbal communications

Each of the above defines the groups to which we belong and from which we form our identity. However, they alone do not do so. Socialization agents, such as the following, also play a significant role in shaping our identities by providing messages that filter and define the groups to which we belong (Cushner, McClelland, & Safford, 2012; Clark, 2013). Those socializing agents include:

- Family

- School
- Clubs and sports
- Media (electronic and print)
- Neighborhood or community
- Peers
- Place of worship

Another way to distinguish the roles of cultural identifiers and socialization agents is that cultural identifiers are the positions held by our students; socialization agents are the vehicles from which those positions gain meaning. This activity allows students to recognize the significance of those positions and meanings and in turn assists students in moving forward in their journey toward multiculturalism.

The purpose of this activity is to assist pre-service teachers in understanding their cultural identities—those socialization agents and cultural identifiers that have shaped who they are. This activity also enhances the possibility that students will realize that they are cultural beings—not the "norm," but products of the people and institutions that shaped them.

LEARNING OBJECTIVES

As a result of this activity, students will:

- take the first step in developing an understanding of their own cultural identity;
- gain an understanding of the cultural identifiers that shape their identity;
- gain an understanding of the socialization agents that shape their identity; and
- begin the process of recognizing that they are simultaneously similar and different from others.

PROCEDURES

1. Have students use Google Chrome to access dlclark7.kent.edu (the program does not work in other web browsers). Upon arriving at this site, the first step is registering. This is done easily by scrolling down the page and registering an account. This information is not recorded as part of the program, so it is important that students keep a record of their user name and password.
2. Once registered, one logs in and begins answering statements that are linked to their cultural identity. A total of 244 statements exist, requiring about thirty minutes to an hour to complete. To view and answer the statements, there are two buttons that can be utilized to make the outer wheel (sources of cultural identity) or inner wheel

(socialization agents) rotate. For each pair (a source of cultural identity and a socialization agent) there are two statements to consider, such as the following:

> **Outer Circle:** *Location*; **Inner Circle:** *School*
> **Question:** Being from the North or South, East Coast, or West Coast and/or being from a city or small town helped shape my experiences in school.
> **Question:** My school helped shape my views of being from the North or South, East Coast, or West Coast and/or being from a city or small town.

3. For each statement the respondent will select "very significant," "significant" or "not significant." Upon answering all statements, the respondent then will click on the "view results" button, and an image of their cultural identity will appear, looking something like the image in figure 20.1 (following page).

   Note: a student will only be able to see the image of their cultural identity after answering a minimum of 100 statements. However, to get a more realistic view of their cultural identity, students should answer all 244 statements.

4. Upon seeing their cultural identity image on the computer screen, students should print it out and bring it to class.

5. The circles on the left (which appear in yellow on the screen) represent the five most significant cultural identifiers in the student's life with increasing size representing more significance; the circles on the right (which appear in blue on the screen) represent the five most significant socialization agents in the student's life with increasing size representing more significance.

6. The lines represent the connections between socialization agents and cultural identifiers, with thicker lines representing stronger connections than thinner lines. Each individual must determine the direction of the connection. For example, for some individuals, his or her gender shapes his or her role in the family; for others, their family defines for them the meaning of their gender. As can be seen in this example, often the connection is bi-directional.

7. Many students need to be prodded to understand their own cultural identity image. For example, "age" may be a cultural identifier that is significant for many students. The following questions could assist them in understanding the significance of age in their life:

   a. Do you spend time primarily with people your own age or do you spend time with people of all ages?

   b. Do you feel that you are much like people your own age or much different?

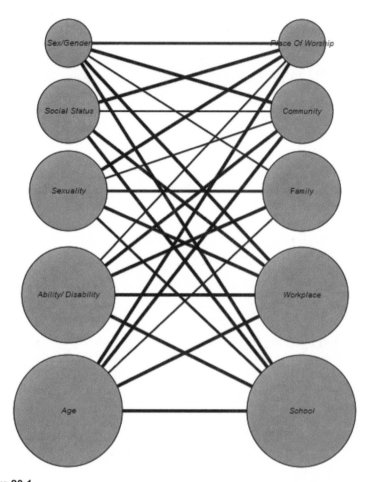

Figure 20.1.

       c. Do you feel that your generation is like previous generations or is it vastly different?

8. The key to this interactive online cultural tool is to recognize that it is not diagnostic in nature; rather, it is a tool to promote discussion.
9. Once each student has an understanding of their cultural identity, in small groups they can discuss their cultural identity image using the following questions to promote discussion:

       a. What surprised you when you first saw the image of your cultural identity?
       b. Do you agree or disagree that the image represents your cultural identity?

    c. How would you redraw your identity to better represent your cultural identity?

    d. The Cultural Learning Process Model consists of more sources of cultural identity and more socialization agents than are in the final diagram; only five of each are shown in your identity image, the five most significant of each. Why do you believe these are represented in your cultural identity image? Which ones that you think are important are missing? Why do you think the ones missing are not in your image?

    e. How does your cultural identity compare to the cultural identity of others? What similarities are evident? What differences are evident? Discuss in your group these similarities and differences.

ADDITIONAL COMMENTS

My classrooms are much like the demographics of teachers—primarily white, primarily middle class, and primarily female. This lack of diversity in the classroom can be a particular challenge when trying to help students in understanding human diversity in education. For many years, I have tried numerous activities to help students understand that they are cultural beings; they are not the "norm," from which others differ or strive to be. It is with this quest in mind that I created the online interactive learning module.

In many respects, I took this activity to an environment where my students felt comfortable, the Internet, and turned the activity into something that simulated the games and activities they play in a medium such as Facebook.

Doing so has piqued student interest. I give students two weeks to answer the questions, but they often return within two days with the images of their cultural identity. They want to know immediately what it means. I often need to meet with them in small groups and ask them questions to help them understand their own cultural identity image. For example, a number of students had "age" as their most significant cultural identifier and did not know why. Upon answering questions, some students realized that age was significant in their lives because they spent very little time around others of different ages; others discovered that age was significant because they spent much of their time with older or younger family members.

The most striking realization for many students was that school was on their list of significant socialization agents, often more significant than family. Through various questions I help them see that their K–12 school experience played a significant role in the development of their cultural identity.

Once I demonstrate asking questions to find out why a student's cultural identity looked as it did, I step away and have students question each other. Doing so helps them not only to realize that they are cultural beings, but that they are not completely the same or completely different from each other, their professors, or their future students (Knefelkamp, 1999).

One note of caution for anyone using this online module: it is a discussion tool, only. It is not diagnostic and should never be used as an assessment. Some students became frustrated with the image of their cultural identity because it did not look as they thought it should. When this happened, I simply asked why they thought that might be the case and told them to redraw the image to how they thought it should look. This, too, adds to the discussion.

REFERENCES

Banks, J. (2012). *Encyclopedia of Diversity in Education, Thousand Oaks*, CA: Sage Publications.

Banks, James A. and Michelle Tucker. (1998) "Multiculturalism's five dimensions." NEA Today Online. Retrieved March 25, 2013, from http://www.learner.org/workshops/socialstudies/pdf/session3/3.Multiculturalism.pdf.

Bennett, M. J. (1993) "Towards ethnorelativism: A developmental model of intercultural sensitivity. In R. M. Paige (ed.) *Education for the Intercultural Experience.* Yarmouth, ME: Intercultural Press.

Clark, D. (2012). *Bias Beneath the facts: Education in a Democratic society.* San Diego: Cognella.

Coleman, W., Professor of Communication and Assistant to the President for Diversity Affairs, Mount Union College, personal correspondence, December 10, 2012.

Cushner, K., McClelland, A. & Safford, P. (2012). *Human diversity in education: An intercultural approach, 7th ed.,* Boston: McGraw-Hill.

Evans, Nancy J., Forney, Deanna S. Guido, Florence M., Patton, Lori D., Renn, Kristen A. *Student Development in College,* San Francisco: John Wiley and Sons p. 92.

Knefelkamp, L. "The influence of a classic." *Liberal Education.* Summer 2003, Vol. 89, no 3, 10.

Knefelkamp, L. (1999) The multicultural curriculum and communities of peace. *Liberal Education,* no. 2, 78, 26.

Perry, W. (1999) Forms of ethical and intellectual development in the college years: A scheme. San Francisco: Jossy Bass, as cited in Knefelkamp, L. "The Influence of a Classic." *Liberal Education.* Summer 2003, Vol. 89, no. 3, 10–15.

Shinnar, Rachel. (2008). Coping with negative social identity: The case of the Mexican immigrants. *The Journal of Social Psychology.* Vol. 148, no. 5, 553–75.

Tajfel, H., & Turner, J. C. (1986). The social identity theory of intergroup behavior. In S. Worchel & W. Austin (Eds.), *The Social Psychology of Intergroup Behavior* (pp. 7–24). Chicago, IL: Nelson Hall.

Activity 21

Who Am I? Exploring Students' Social Identities and Social Inequalities in Cultural Contexts

Jennifer L. Fisette

ABSTRACT

People's identities are socially constructed and shaped by such forces as schools, communities, and the world in which we live. Who you are and how you identify yourself impacts who you are as a teacher. Often, we as people and as teachers do not understand or know the basis of our views, beliefs, stereotypes, and biases.

For us to have a true sense of who we are and to have the capability and awareness to know our students for who they are, we first must identify our own privileges and/or how we are marginalized and then deconstruct our socially constructed stereotypes and biases. Ultimately, we want our students to be empowered by taking part in a democratic process that guides them to uncover and explore social inequalities and develop as literate and critical consumers of sport, physical activity, and the movement culture.

BACKGROUND AND PURPOSE

Within research on the context of physical education, identity has been considered in the ways that physical education curricula and teacher education programs may be serving to support cultural identities, which work to create boundaries and maintain inequality (e.g., Beckett, 2004; Dowling, 2008; Dowling & Karhus, 2011; Tinning, 2004; Wrench & Garrett, 2012). This body of work exposes what has been termed the "hidden curriculum," whereby schools create contexts that teach far more than the content stated within official academic curricula (Bain, 1990).

Hidden curricula are ways educators, often without intention, promote ideologies about such things as race, gender, and sexuality, which might serve to further inequalities and divisions that are disempowering for students. Without conscious attempts to understand and expose the hidden curriculum, such disempowering ideologies are supported and maintained, rather than questioned and deconstructed. Scholars have addressed this and recommended strategies on creating a more inclusive and equitable educational experience to empower students within and outside of educational contexts (e.g., Fisette, 2011, 2013; Fisette & Walton, in press; Tinning, 2004).

Importantly, scholars have examined embodied identities within physical education contexts, interrogating the processes through which identities and the ideologies associated with them are understood and performed (e.g., Azzarito, 2009; Azzarito & Katzew, 2010; Fisette, 2011; Oliver & Lalik, 2001, 2004). These studies make explicit the social construction and navigation of cultural identities. Most importantly for this present work, how one physically lives and enacts one's sense of self (i.e., embodied identity), clearly comes to the fore in the body-centered context of physical education.

Thus, the purpose of these activities is to provide participants with the opportunity to explore their sense of self and embodied identities within a variety of cultural contexts that they live in, know, and understand and those they have yet to experience. Through this exploration as well as engaged discourse, the goal is for the participants to not only increase their understanding of their own selves, but to also gain awareness and potential acceptance of those individuals who are similar to and/or different from them.

LEARNING OBJECTIVES

The focus and emphasis on exploring one's sense of self, embodied identities, and social inequalities is an important process for all participants, specifically, teacher candidates. Potential changes in one's beliefs, perspectives, and stereotypes need time to develop and evolve; thus, it is important for participants to have ample opportunities to engage in activities that emphasize their social identity as well as expose social inequalities. In the process section, numerous activities are described, all of which can be infused in courses throughout a participant's teacher education program, including introduction/foundations, content, and teacher preparation courses.

Participants will:

- critically examine their sense of self and social identity within the cultural context that they live in, know, and understand;

- engage in discourse about social inequalities and reflect upon/provide examples when their identity was placed in a position of power (i.e., privilege) or in a marginalized position;
- construct a social identity profile and/or social identity paper;
- read and respond to their peers' stories; and
- reflect upon their experiences in engaging in this explorative process of their embodied identities and social inequalities, and identify the importance of their social identity, beliefs, stereotypes, and overall social inequalities as future teachers.

PROCEDURE

Introduction/Foundations Courses

Participants will:

1. Complete a social identity profile with predetermined socially constructed categories.
2. Respond to the following questions:

   a. Using the social identities listed above that apply to you (i.e., how you identify as a person), on the left side of this sheet create a pie chart or diagram to show which identities are most important to you. Then, create a pie chart or diagram that shows which identities you think about the most.
   b. Reflect upon how you felt completing this social identity profile.

3. Discuss, in small groups their social identities, how they came to their social identities, and what they learned about one another.
4. View "A Class Divided," the Jane Elliot Experiment (YouTube clip, developed in 1970).
5. Reflect upon their experiences in viewing "A Class Divided" (via "think, pair, share").

   a. What were you feeling as you watched this video?
   b. What was the purpose of this experiment?
   c. What did you learn from this experiment?
   d. How does this experiment have meaning to you as a future professional?

Content and Methods Courses (Undergraduate and Graduate)

1. Participants will write a reflective paper that explores their own sense of social identity as well as how their family, school, work, and/or social and religious experiences have contributed to the de-

velopment of that identity. They will also describe how their perceived embodied identity has developed/changed over time. Reflective questions are provided as prompts.

2. Inform participants that their classmates will view their paper so it is important to take this into consideration as they write their paper. That is, they should share to the level of their comfort, be thoughtful, and allow others to learn more about who they are.

3. Make the social identity papers available to all participants (e.g., upload to a course communication tool such as Blackboard, Vista; send them as e-mail attachments, or have participants read them aloud in class).

4. Write your own social identity paper, as the instructor of the course, and make it available after the other participants have submitted their papers.

5. Have the participants read each of their classmates' social identity papers. If desired (based on number of participants and how the papers have been available to them), have the participants respond/reflect upon each of the identity papers.

6. Participants will then write a reflective response paper about their own process in writing their identity paper (and perhaps may include more here), their experience in reading their classmates' papers, and finally, what they learned about themselves and others throughout this identity exploration.

7. Engage in small group and whole class discussion about who they are, what they learned, and the importance of reflecting upon and exploring one's social identity as well as social inequalities. Tie in the discussion to why it is important for them to have an understanding and awareness of social identities and social inequalities as future teachers.

8. Throughout the course while participants are in field experiences, have them identify social inequalities in the schools, the physical education program, and specifically in their class. Discuss how they handled the situation: did they perpetuate the social inequality and the hidden curriculum or educate students about the inequality that was exposed in class?

ADDITIONAL COMMENTS

In the introduction/foundations courses, the students tend to be what I call "tipped upside down" when I ask them to discuss and reflect upon their social identity. Usually they are much more open to discuss social identities and inequalities after we watch the "Class Divided" videos. I cover this topic within the first few weeks of the semester, but we discuss social issues and inequalities throughout the course, which gives the students repetition and time to develop greater understanding and awareness of their own identities as well as the identities of others.

I go into greater depth with my students in the content and methods courses by having them complete the assignments out of class over the weekend where they upload their work to our university online learning center. It is always interesting to see how everyone looks at one another and what the class sounds like when we meet for the first time after they complete the assignment.

The students are usually taken aback at how much they thought they knew about classmates with whom they had taken classes for years, yet find out very personal information about each of them. The students feel it brings the class closer, because they all make themselves vulnerable, including the instructor, and have a better understanding, awareness, and appreciation for inclusiveness of all individuals. Once they begin their field experiences, they are much more open and aware to students' social identities and social inequalities in their classes.

REFERENCES

Azzarito, L. (2009). The panopticon of physical education: Pretty, active and ideally white. *Physical Education and Sport Pedagogy*, 14(1), 19–39.

Azzarito, L., & Katzew, A. (2010). Performing identities in physical education: (En)gendering fluid selves. *Research Quarterly for Exercise & Sport*, 81(1), 25–37.

Bain, L. L. (1990). A critical analysis of the hidden curriculum in physical education. In D. Kirk & R. Tinning (Eds.), *Physical education, curriculum, and culture: Critical issues in the contemporary crisis* (pp. 23–42). London: The Farmer Press.

Beckett, L. (2004). Editorial: Health, the body, and identity work in health and physical education. *Sport, Education & Society*, 9(2), 171–73.

Dowling, F. (2008). Getting in touch with our feelings: The emotional geographies of gender relations in PETE. *Sport, Education & Society*, 13(3), 247–66.

Dowling, F., & Karhus, S. (2011). An analysis of the ideological work of the discourses of "fair play" and moral education in perpetuating inequitable gender practices in PETE. *Physical Education & Sport Pedagogy*, 16(2), 197–211.

Fisette, J. L. (2013). "Are you listening?": Adolescent girls voice how they negotiate self-identified barriers to their success and survival in physical education. *Physical Education and Sport Pedagogy*, 18(2), 184–203.

Fisette, J. L. (2011). Exploring how girls navigate their embodied identities in physical education. *Physical Education and Sport Pedagogy*, 16(2), 179–96.

Fisette, J. L., & Walton, T. A. (in press for print publication; December 2011, electronic publication). "If you really knew me". . . I am empowered through action. *Sport, Education and Society*.

Jane Elliot Experiment—Part I. (n.d.). Retrieved from http://www.youtube.com/watch?v=JCjDxAwfXV0.

Jane Elliot Experiment—Part II. (n.d.). Retrieved from http://www.youtube.com/watch?v=0UbNp15zDtE&feature=related.

Oliver, K. L., & Lalik, R. (2001). The body as curriculum: Learning with adolescent girls. *Journal of Curriculum Studies*, 33(3), 303–33.

Oliver, K. L., & Lalik, R. (2004). "The beauty walk": Interrogating whiteness as the norm for beauty within one school's hidden curriculum. In J. Evans, B. Davies, & J. Wright (Eds.), *Body Knowledge and Control: Studies in the Sociology of Physical Education and Health* (pp. 115–29). New York: Routledge.

Tinning, R. (2004). Rethinking the preparation of HPE teachers: Ruminations on knowledge, identity, and ways of thinking. *Asia-Pacific Journal of Teacher Education, 32*(3), 241–53.

Wrench, A., & Garrett, R. (2012). Identity work: Stories told in learning to teach physical education. *Sport, Education & Society, 17*(1), 1–19.

Activity 22

Bricks in a Backpack: Respecting the Invisible

Diane M. Vetter

ABSTRACT

This lesson provides teacher candidates with insights into the often invisible social and emotional issues that burden young children and impact their ability to learn effectively in the classroom. Using the analogy of carrying a brick in the backpack, the author facilitates the understanding for teacher candidates that issues of low student engagement, classroom behaviors, and lack of interest in learning may be the result of social and emotional burdens carried by young learners.

PURPOSE AND BACKGROUND

As an elementary classroom teacher, every Tuesday after Labor Day I watched the children arrive for the first time in my elementary school classroom. I noticed the bulging backpacks that each of them carried. Some backpacks were bright and new, sporting the logo of the latest cartoon character, sports team, or designer. Others were battered and worn. Every backpack contained a collection of items that were special to the owner. Some had a selection of pencils and markers. Some held a favorite toy. Most, but not all, held a lunch or snack for the day. Always a wide array of articles was carried into my classroom each day.

As I got to know my new students each year, I would begin to notice that in addition to their heavy backpacks, many of my students carried other burdens to school each day. Although these burdens were invisible to the casual observer, their impact was great and served to marginalize the students who carried them in a multitude of ways.

Some students carried burdens of social weight—racism, bullying, poverty, broken homes, or abusive parents. Other students carried the weight of emotional or cognitive burdens—depression, issues of self-esteem, and learning challenges. Each of these burdens greatly influenced how a child learned, interacted, and engaged in my classroom.

Darling-Hammond, French, and Garcia-Lopez (2002) remarked on the challenge of discussing issues of social justice with teacher candidates (TCs) "who had little personal experience with the issues of inequity, marginalization, discrimination, and oppression that are regularly experienced by students whose race, income, language, sexuality or learning abilities place them outside the mainstream" (p. 2). I experienced similar challenges; I struggled to make explicit the concept of marginalization to groups of teacher candidates whose academic success in secondary school had gained them entry into a highly competitive and well-respected teacher education program.

To help my teacher candidates understand that if they wanted to be successful in facilitating learning for all children, they needed to know much more about their students than their cultural background, learning style, or achievement level. Therefore, I decided to use a visualization of my students' invisible burdens as heavy bricks in the backpacks that the children carried to my class each day. I have since facilitated this lesson in many classrooms and shared it with my colleagues who have done likewise. Years later, it continues to be the one lesson that teacher candidates talk about when they share stories of their own classrooms.

I refer to the lesson as Bricks in the Backpack: Respecting the Invisible. The following is my lesson outline.

Lesson Outline

To prepare for the lesson, I wrap enough bricks in white paper to be able to distribute one per group. I then label each brick with an issue that has impacted a child in my classroom. Although I never identify my former students, I personalize each issue to allow teacher candidates to hear the children's voices and understand that we are talking about real children rather than faceless social issues or learning challenges. The following list provides a few examples of the text that might appear on a brick.

- I didn't sleep much last night. My parents were fighting and screaming.
- I didn't have any breakfast today and there is no lunch in my backpack.
- The cops took my mom away and I have to stay with my grandma.
- I hate recess. The other kids bully me all the time.
- I can't read, but nobody knows. I am real good at pretending.
- I take dance, piano, voice, and gymnastics. My mom says I could be a star so I have to practice all the time.

- I'm only 10 but I am responsible for my 3 little sisters. My mom sleeps all the time.

I open the lesson with a read aloud of Patricia Polacco's (1998), *Thank You, Mr. Falker*. This is an autobiographical story of the author's experience as a child who was bullied due to her inability to read. The story builds a context for the lesson to follow. It is also important that this story is autobiographical. The teacher candidates need to personalize the lesson by putting a face on a situation. A strictly theoretical study removes the empathy that I believe is required to fully internalize the key learnings.

After we read the story, I ask teacher candidates to reflect on how they learn and how they do NOT learn. This focuses the lesson on the individuality of successful learning. The next step is to ask teacher candidates to visualize a child they know, or perhaps themselves as a child. They proceed to "bring the child to life" for a partner, by describing the child's personal characteristics. Based on their understanding of that child, together the partners then brainstorm ways that they might effectively engage that child in learning. Partners then briefly share their thoughts within the small group. The teacher candidate has now expanded his or her context from self to other.

For the second part of the activity I distribute a backpack with a brick inside to each group. I often do this activity at the beginning of the school year. In that case, the day prior I ask the teacher candidates to bring one small new item to contribute to a backpack for a child who may not have one. I ask friends or family to help me collect new backpacks. Then at the end of the lesson we donate the filled backpacks to a local charitable organization. Other times, I simply collect some old backpacks, put a labeled brick in each and distribute one to each group.

Prior to opening the backpacks, I ask the teacher candidates to speculate on what they might expect to find inside. We make a list of all the weird and wonderful things that children keep in their backpacks. When it comes time to open the backpacks, the students are surprised to find the bricks inside. I explain how I have come to visualize the burdens that my students carry as *weights* that wear them down each and every day.

I ask teacher candidates to equate the physical burden of carrying a heavy weight to the emotional and/or psychological burden of carrying one or more of the *issues* on the brick. It is often the children who carry one of these burdens to school who find themselves ostracized by their peers, thereby adding an additional *brick* to their load.

Once the TCs have removed the bricks from the backpacks, I distribute chart paper or a whiteboard and ask each group to brainstorm how the effects of carrying that specific *brick* daily might manifest itself on classroom behavior and learning. Typical responses include: homework incomplete, lethargy, disinterest, disengagement, acting out, bullying, and so forth.

As each group discusses the issue on their brick, I circulate to answer questions and add in some details to reinforce that each of these issues represents a real story from my teaching experience. I explain that it is crucial for them to understand that these are not hypothetical situations, reality TV tales, or fiction; these are authentic stories of real children who have crossed my path. This part of the lesson usually takes about sixty minutes as teacher candidates become engaged in the discussion and begin to reflect back on their experience as classroom volunteers, educational assistants, camp counselors, and so forth.

Teacher Candidates often "wonder" about children they have encountered and rethink their reactions and those of other adults to children who carry *bricks* in their backpacks. They begin to question the snap judgments that teachers may make about a child's behavior or lack of engagement in the classroom when they don't fully understand the burdens that the child carries. Inevitably, this leads to much shared empathy, and perhaps feelings of not having done enough for a child they have known.

As the group discussions wind down, I usually move into a fifteen-minute break as some of the discussions may have been emotional for some teacher candidates. When the class reconvenes, I ask them to share a synopsis of their discussion with the other groups in a whole-class sharing session. They quickly come to a consensus that there is much that may have gone unnoticed in classrooms where they have worked or studied.

I always end the lesson with a "soliloquy." As I begin, I ask them to take turns holding the brick from the backpack in one hand, with that hand extended. I ask them to hold that brick until their arm tires, then pass it on to their neighbor until the brick has made its way around the group.

As they bear the weight of the brick in one hand, I tell them that they are privileged. They have been academically successful (certainly many of them have struggled to achieve what they have and I acknowledge that). Nevertheless, today they sit in the Faculty of Education classroom as successful learners. They are in the classroom because they want to be there. They may be challenged by the workload of the course, but they know that their past success in academic work means that they are likely to succeed.

In contrast, I remind them of the children who carry these *bricks* in their backpacks. They may come to the classroom with the overwhelming fear or "knowledge" that they will not succeed. They have likely been unsuccessful in classrooms before. Unlike teacher candidates who can decide that maybe this program is not for them, children in the classroom do not have that option. Day after day, month after month, they must come to school every day. They may feel that they are destined to fail, yet they have no choice but to come back each day to relive that experience.

I quote a principal at my school board who referred to these children as heroes. I ask the teacher candidates to contemplate how many of us would return day after day to something when we felt we were doomed to fail. How many of us would have the courage to continue with a task that was so overwhelming, so frightening, so daunting, that it made us anxious, physically ill, or emotionally distressed every day? I admit that I do not believe that I could be so brave.

I ask my TCs to stop and reflect on the children in their host classrooms, to think about the conversations they may have overheard in staff rooms about these children. Are they really "behavior problems," "pains in the neck," or "aggravations?" I tell them unequivocally, "NO." These children are heroes who come back day after day only to be emotionally beaten down again and again.

These children deserve our compassion, our understanding, and our advocacy. We need to be their champions. We need to stand in admiration of their determination, to walk with them to help them find their rightful place in the world. We need to stand up for them when no one else seems ready to do so. We celebrate other heroes so easily in our society. It is time to celebrate these young heroes, too!

REFERENCES

Darling-Hammond, L., French, J., & Garcia-Lopez, S. P. (Eds.). (2002). *Learning to Teach for Social Justice*. New York: Teachers College Press.

Polacco, P. (1998). *Thank you, Mr. Falker*. New York: Philomel.

Activity 23

Preservice Teachers Are Students, Too: Developing Awareness of White Identity and Privilege to Facilitate Change for Inclusivity and Equality

Tracy Lara

ABSTRACT

Increasing diversity among school children in Pre-K–12 has not been matched by diversity among preservice teachers (Banks & Banks, 2001). These overall homogenous preservice teacher cohorts have also been characterized as unprepared and/or lacking the awareness, knowledge, and skills to teach with cultural sensitivity and competency (Milner et al., 2003). Milner et al. stated "many preservice teachers have never had significant interactions with students from diverse backgrounds" (p. 63). As a result, these teachers are unable to challenge the systemic racism persistent in the American educational hierarchies.

It is clear that teacher education programs must prepare teachers to meet the learning needs of diverse students, and furthermore, teachers must assist students from dominant groups to develop dispositions and skills enabling them to successfully interact and collaborate with others across differences (Banks, 2001).

BACKGROUND AND PURPOSE

Multiculturalism has been traditionally, if at all, presented to preservice teachers with a focus on marginalized students (Cobham, 2011). Unfortunately, this approach may perpetuate a deficit cognitive frame (Bensimon, 2005) in guiding how educators view these students.

A cognitive frame is the way an individual understands or interprets a phenomenon (Bensimon, 2005). Bensimon described individuals operating from a deficit cognitive frame as those who may value diversity, yet attribute differential educational outcomes for disenfranchised students to negative factors or stereotypes reifying the status quo. Cobham suggested that educating education practitioners about white privilege and white identity development may arouse awareness of the role of race in students' educational experience as well as preservice teacher awareness of their own privilege and how that may influence interactions in the classroom.

Curriculum that focuses on issues of power, privilege, and oppression encourage transformative learning that empowers students to reflect upon and to take action to initiate change (Banks, 2001). The activity in this chapter is designed to increase preservice teachers' awareness of white privilege and white identity development and may be modified for use in teaching students about white privilege and identity development.

Educating students about the history of their own heritage and culture is a commonly used approach to increase appreciation of differences. The greater majority of white graduate students I have taught either can point to some tradition passed down from their grandparents, or they more commonly state, "I have no culture, I'm American." Because students equate traditional dress or foods with culture, they are like fish in the pond, unable to see their own culture all around them. Similarly, they have a fascination with the differences they see beyond the safe protection of the glass bowl barrier.

In a related fashion, most students are unaware of the history of white Americans in the United States, which further clouds their awareness of heritage and culture. As a result, they do not recognize their white privilege or the systems around them that oppress nonwhites. Since this is the case of white graduate students I have taught in three distinct regions of the United States, I can only suppose that undergraduates with even less life experience are likewise unaware of their history, culture, and privilege, much less their own whiteness and how that interplays in their personal and professional interactions.

LEARNING OBJECTIVES

Three steps are necessary to mobilize students to gain awareness of their racial identity development, a crucial process equipping individuals to challenge structures perpetuating oppression. These steps are arousal, reflection, and interaction. The purpose of this activity, thus, is to provide the scaffolding to increase student awareness of their own racial identity and to situate that awareness in their personalized context of becoming an educator. Through this activity students will:

- define racism, privilege, and oppression from a systems perspective in order to identify and discuss educational structures that may contribute to perpetuating or dismantling racism in education;
- reflect on their own identity development as related to Social Identity Development Theory (Hardiman & Jackson, 1997; see Appendix) and discuss their own experience with privilege and oppression; and
- participate in conversations to examine how students' previous experiences and learning influence interactions with whites and non-whites in our increasingly multicultural society.

PROCESS

The objectives can be accomplished in three sequential 45-minute to 1-hour sessions. Students will typically have been assigned reading or video viewing prior to the class session (see Sequenced Assigned Reading below). Lynn and Smith-Maddox (2007) asserted, "through dialogue which promotes reflection, teachers can move towards a fuller understanding of the ways in which they can unravel the complexities of their own beliefs about their students as well as the demands of teaching in diverse contexts" (p. 98).

Students will have been assigned to groups of six and will remain with those groups for each of the three sessions. For each session, two of the students will be assigned to co-lead the interaction dialogue component of the lesson on a rotational basis, such that each student co-leads one of the discussions in the sequence. It is recommended that, in the week preceding the sequence, students be provided with a brief group orientation of approximately 25 minutes in which students are given a 5-minute overview of group leadership and are assembled in their groups to make introductions and set ground rules.

Online resources such as http://www.wikihow.com/Lead-a-Discussion may be provided to students as guidelines for how to lead the group discussion. At this time, remind students to assemble their chairs in a circle facing each other and without any table or desk in the center or between any group members.

During each class session in the sequence, the instructor will provide a brief (10–15 minute) review of key concepts, definitions, or questions from the assigned reading and/or video. Students will assemble into their assigned groups for a 30-minute discussion led by the assigned group leaders. The instructor will circulate among the groups to gain a sense of the direction and topics being discussed and will provide a 5-minute caution to allow group leaders to bring the groups to closure.

The instructor will then use the remaining time to lead a class discussion highlighting the points discussed as related to the objectives and applications to teaching practice fostering interactions with students, colleagues, and administrators across differences to create inclusive and equitable learning environments. Possible questions for the class discussion include:

1. What idea most impacted your thinking from your group discussions?
2. In your own words define these terms and provide an example from your experience that illustrates the term: privilege, racism, oppression.
3. How can you apply an idea from your discussion to what you have experienced, or observed in classrooms, to create a more inclusive and equitable learning environment?
4. Based on your discussion, what action can you take to make your classroom more multiculturally sensitive or equitable?

Students may be assigned to write a reflection paper about how participating in the interaction dialogue has informed their thinking and planned actions for teaching practice, classroom management, and advocating and action taking to achieve equitable classrooms and schools.

SEQUENCED ASSIGNED READING

Using these suggested resources and others, students are introduced to content pertaining to white identity development (Cobham, 2011); privilege and oppression (Johnson, 2006; McIntosh, 2003); Social Identity Development Theory (Hardiman & Jackson, 1997; Howard-Hamilton & Hinton, 2011); and teaching practices for social action (Marshall & Klein, 2009). The motion picture *Gangs in New York* (Grimaldi, Weinstein, Weinstein, & Scorcese (2002) offers a fictitious portrayal of white immigration to the United States. Use the following content sequence for the three group sessions.

Session 1 Assigned Reading and Viewing

Cobham (2011), pp. 213–26. This selected reading presents race as a social construction that determines social, economic, and political status in the United States and influences interactions between and among whites and nonwhites on college campuses. Cobham provides definitions of systemic racism and oppression. Optionally, instructors may assign students to view *Gangs in New York* (Grimaldi et al., 2002) or may use a clip from this movie in the overview and preface to the interaction discussions.

Session 2 Assigned Reading

Johnson (2006). Select chapters or assign the entire book. This is a quick and accessible read that enables students to understand privilege and oppression and the systems and power structures that perpetuate inequality. Optionally, the instructor may assign McIntosh (2003) or use key points from the essay in the overview as a preface to the interaction discussions.

Session 3 Assigned Reading

Marshall and Klein (2009); Howard-Hamilton and Hinton (2001), pp. 26–27 and/or Hardiman & Jackson (1997). Optionally, use the handout that follows to provide an overview of the Social Identity Development Theory (Hardiman & Jackson, 1997) to preface the interaction discussions.

APPENDIX

Social Identity Development Theory (Hardiman & Jackson, 1997)

- Indicates characteristics common to identity development of oppressed and dominant groups
- Individuals may be in multiple stages simultaneously as they cope with different cognitive and emotional struggles with oppression
- Useful in understanding the perspectives of students and informing programming

DEFINITIONS

- Privilege—unearned advantages and benefits granted to people in the dominant group
- Oppression—pervasive inequality manifest through the devaluing of a social group, consciously or subconsciously, by another social group for that group's gain (Hardiman & Jackson, 1997).

STAGES

- **Naïve/no social consciousness**—"individuals unaware of the complex codes of appropriate behavior for members of their social group" (Hardiman & Jackson, p. 23).
- **Acceptance**—roles prescribed by influential others (e.g., parents, teachers, clergy, or media) are internalized. Conscious or unconscious conformity to characteristics imposed by society.

- **Resistance**—increased awareness, typically through a challenging life event that creates dissonance for dominant group members. The oppressed acknowledge and question the damaging effects associated with the collective experiences of oppression.
- **Redefinition**—creation of a new identity
- **Internalization**—infusing the newly defined self into every aspect of one's life.

	Dominant	Oppressed
Passive Acceptance	"Have to some degree internalized codes of appropriate behavior, [so] conscious effort is no longer required to remind them of what to do and how to think" (Hardiman & Jackson, p. 24)	"Oblivious to how they emulate the oppressor and reflect the oppressor's views" (Howard-Hamilton & Hinton, 2011, p. 26).
Active Acceptance	Overt and direct messages are received that portray oppressed people as weak, inferior, or deviant.	"Have learned to internalize and accept messages about the inferiority of their culture and themselves and overtly or consciously connect with the views, beliefs, and ideology of the dominant group" (Howard-Hamilton & Hinton, 2011, p. 26).

Table 23.1.

REFERENCES

Banks, J. A. (2001). *Cultural diversity and education: Foundations, curriculum and teaching.* Boston: Allyn and Bacon.

Banks, J. A., & Banks, C. A. M. (Eds.). (2001). *Multicultural Education: Issues & Perspectives* (4th ed.). New York: Wiley.

Bensimon, E. M. (2005). Closing the achievement gap in higher education: An organizational learning perspective. *New Directions for Higher Education, 131,* 99–111.

Cobham, B. A. M. (2011). White college students. In M. J. Cuyjet, M. F. Howard-Hamilton, & D. L., Cooper (Eds.), *Multiculturalism on Campus: Theory, Models, and Practices for Understanding Diversity and Creating Inclusion* (pp. 213–36). Sterling, VA: Stylus.

Grimaldi, A., Weinstein, H., & Weinstein, B. (Producers), & Scorcese, M. (Director). (2002). *Gangs of New York* [Motion Picture]. United States & Italy: Miramax Films.

Hardiman, R., & Jackson, B. W. (1997). Conceptual foundation for social justice courses. In M. Adams, L. A. Bell, & P. Griffin (Eds.), *Teaching for Diversity and Social Justice: A Sourcebook* (pp. 16–29). New York: Routledge.

Howard-Hamilton, M. F., & Hinton, K. G. (2011). Oppression and its effect on college student identity development. In M. J. Cuyjet, M. F. Howard-Hamilton, & D. L. Cooper (Eds.), *Multiculturalism on Campus: Theory, Models, and Practices for Understanding Diversity and Creating Inclusion* (pp. 19–36). Sterling, VA: Stylus.

Johnson, A. G. (2006). *Privilege, Power, and Difference* (2nd ed). Boston: McGraw-Hill.

Lynn, M., & Smith-Maddox, R. (2007). Preservice teacher inquiry: Creating space to dialogue about becoming a social justice educator. *Teaching and Teacher Education, 23,* 94–105.

Marshall, J. & Klein, A. M. (2009). Lessons in social action: Equipping and inspiring students to improve their world. *The Social Studies*, 218–21.

McIntosh, P. (2003). White privilege: Unpacking the invisible knapsack. In S. Pious (Ed.), *Understanding prejudice and discrimination* (pp. 191–96). New York: McGraw-Hill.

Milner, R. H., Fowers, L. A., Moore, E., & Moore, J. L. (2003). Preservice teachers' awareness of multiculturalism and diversity. *The High School Journal, 87*(1), 63–70.

Contributing Authors

Joanne Caniglia teaches mathematics education at Kent State University. Her research includes special education and mathematics. She enjoys bringing theory into practice for teachers and future teachers.

Debra L. Clark is an associate professor in cultural foundations of education. Her research focus is the connection of personality traits of preservice teachers to openness to issues of diversity.

Kenneth Cushner, Ed.D., is professor of international and intercultural teacher education at Kent State University, author of numerous textbooks, chapters, and articles in the fields of multicultural education and intercultural training, and a founding fellow and past president of the International Academy for Intercultural Research. He also serves as director of the Consortium for Overseas Student Teaching (COST).

Frans H. Doppen, associate professor of social studies education at Ohio University, is the current president of the International Assembly of the National Council for the Social Studies. His research interests focus on global and civic education.

Juliann Dorff is an associate lecturer of art education at Kent State University. Her area of research focuses on teaching art to all children.

Joanne Kilgour Dowdy is a professor of adolescent/adult literacy at Kent State University in the School of Teaching, Learning, and Curriculum Studies. Her major research interests include women and literacy, drama in education, and video technology in qualitative research instruction.

Jennifer L. Fisette is an assistant professor at Kent State University in the Physical Education Teacher Education program. Her scholarship explores the critical examination of embodied identities within physical education through student voice.

Schea N. Fissel, M.A., CCC-SLP is a practicing speech-language pathologist at Kaiser Permanente and doctoral student at Kent State University in the department of Speech Pathology and Audiology. She has research interests in autism, augmentative/alternative communication, and literacy.

Jason C. Fitzgerald, Ph.D. is an assistant professor at Wagner College. He teaches social studies and general education courses with a focus on civic engagement.

Nancy P. Gallavan, professor, University of Central Arkansas, specializes in social studies, cultural competence, and classroom assessments and is active in the Association of Teacher Educators.

Rajlakshmi (Raj) Ghosh is a doctoral student of curriculum and instruction majoring in science education at Kent State University. Originally from the City of Joy-Kolkata, India, she is passionate about inquiry-based science teaching and enjoys reading and travel.

Alyse C. Hachey, Ph.D., is professor and deputy chair at Borough of Manhattan Community College-City University of New York, where she teaches early childhood education curriculum courses.

Matthew S. Hollstein, is a social studies teacher at Columbus Alternative High School (Ohio) and a doctoral candidate in social studies education at Ohio University and is interested in environmental citizenship.

Dr. Paul Kriese, Indiana University East, is interested in the political ramifications of the constitution and efforts to promote diversity and globalization.

Janice Kroeger, Ph.D., is associate professor of early childhood education at Kent State University. Her work focuses on issues of reconceptualizing early childhood research and practice highlighting identity, justice, and equity in education.

Dr. Chia-Ling Kuo is an assistant professor of instructional technology at Kent State University and has collaborated with more than thirty international classes in thirteen countries on the global learning wiki activity since 2011.

Tracy M. Lara, Ph.D., assistant professor of higher education and student personnel and a career counselor, teaches student development and multicultural education courses at Kent State University.

Martha Lash, Ph.D., is an associate professor of early childhood education at Kent State University. Research and teaching interests include teachers' professional development and young children's social development.

April A. Mattix, Ph.D., is an assistant professor at George Mason University where she teaches international education, elementary education, and International Baccalaureate courses.

Yolanda Medina, Ph.D., is associate professor at the Borough of Manhattan Community College-City University of New York where she teaches social foundations of education and art education courses.

Monica Miller Marsh is associate professor of early childhood education and director of the Child Development Center at Kent State University. She is co-founder of the nonprofit Family Diversity Education Council.

Randall E. Osborne, Texas State University-San Marcos, focuses his scholarship on how to maximize learning in online courses and prepare students to think in ways that promote globalization.

JoAnn Phillion is professor of curriculum studies at Purdue University. Her research interests include immigrant student education in Asia and preservice teachers' development in Honduras.

Jubin Rahatzad is a curriculum studies doctoral student at Purdue University, and has an M.A. in political science. Research interests include postglobal and decolonial theories.

Sara Raven is an assistant professor of science education at Kent State University. Her research interests include school bullying, feminist science education, and metacognition.

Keith H. Sakuda, Ph.D., is assistant professor of management at the University of Hawaii, West Oahu. He teaches international business, business ethics, and entrepreneurship.

Hannah Sasser is a doctoral student in curriculum studies at Purdue University, and has a Masters of Education in school counseling from Purdue University.

Suniti Sharma teaches methods courses in the Department of Teacher Education, Saint Joseph's University, Philadelphia. Her research interests include at-risk youth, literacy, and preservice teacher preparation.

Dr. Diane Vetter is the practicum coordinator at York University, Faculty of Education and a former elementary classroom teacher with Simcoe Muskoka Catholic District School Board.

Sofia Villenas is associate professor in the Department of Anthropology and director of the Latino Studies Program at Cornell University. She has served as co-editor of the *Anthropology of Education Quarterly*, and continues to serve as associate editor for the *Journal of Latinos and Education*.